D0976966

you have 82
new messages

A Gift For:

From:

THE

BIBLE ANSWER

BOOK

for students

HANK HANEGRAAFF

the bible answer man

Published by
THOMAS NELSON
Since 1798

For other products and live events, visit us at:
www.thomasnelson.com

The Bible Answer Book for Students
Copyright © 2007 by Hank Hanegraaff
Published by Thomas Nelson, Inc., Nashville, Tennessee 37214

All rights reserved. No portion of this publication may be reproduced, stored in a retrieval system or transmitted in any form by any means—electronic, mechanical, photocopying, recording, or any other—except for brief quotations in printed reviews, without the prior written permission of the publisher.

Unless otherwise indicated, all Scriptures are from the Holy Bible, New International Version®. Copyright © 1973, 1978, 1984 by International Bible Society. Used by permission of Zondervan. All rights reserved.

Other Scriptures are taken from:
The New American Standard Bible (NASB) © 1960, 1962, 1963, 1971, 1972, 1973, 1975, 1977, 1995 by The Lockman Foundation. Used by permission. The King James Version of the Bible (KJV). The New King James Version (NKJV) © 1979, 1980, 1982, 1992, Thomas Nelson, Inc., Publisher. Used by permission.

Project Developer: Lisa Stilwell
Project Editor: Steffany Woolsey Creative Services
Designed by The DesignWorks Group, Sisters, Oregon

ISBN 10: 1–4041–0450–X
ISBN 13: 978–1–4041–0450–1

Printed and bound in China

www.thomasnelson.com
www.equip.org

To John Mark

—your thoughtful questions
on our trip to Florida impassioned
The Bible Answer Book for Students project.
My prayer is that your conversations will always be
"full of grace, seasoned with salt, so that you may
know how to answer everyone" (Colossians 4:6).

Table of Contents

Introduction

Today's teens are giving up on Christianity, and a primary reason can be summed up in two words—*intellectual uncertainty*. Teens are not certain God created the universe; they are not certain the Bible has more authority than the Book of Mormon or the Qur'an; and they are uncertain whether Jesus is God or merely a teacher standing in a long line of peers with Buddha, Muhammad, and Krishna.

The good news is that teens are all ears when it comes to credible answers that fill the void of intellectual uncertainty. And that is not mere speculation! I have experienced the certainty of this contention, first with my own children (I have nine), and then with teens I have had the privilege to engage in conversation for some two decades. Indeed, this is the very reason I am so stoked about providing a student edition of *The Bible Answer Book*. In it, I provide answers to the difficult questions that have stumbled student seekers and solidified student skeptics in their opposition to the Christian worldview.

In *The Bible Answer Book for Students*, I address relevant questions such as, "Is the Bible Outdated in Its Views on Homosexuality?" "Who Made God?" "What Is Truth?" "Don't All Religions Lead to God?" "What Makes Christianity the One True Religion?"

"What Does It Mean to Interpret the Bible Literally?" "How Can We Be Sure That Evolution Is a Myth?" "What's Wrong with Wicca?" and "Should Abortion Be Allowed in Certain Situations, Like Rape or Incest?" In each case I have chiseled my answer until only the gem emerges. Additionally, I provide recommended resources for further study.

It is my prayer that God will use the answers to such questions to not only stem the exodus of teens from Christianity, but to transform them into vigilant contenders "for the faith that was once for all entrusted to the saints" (Jude 3).

–1–

How Can I Be Sure I'm Saved?

This question is the most important one you'll ever ask yourself. No one gets out of this world alive! Even the Bible itself was written "so that you may know that you have eternal life" (1 John 5:13).

So how can you be sure you're saved?

First, according to Scripture, you need to *realize* that you are a sinner. If you don't realize you're a sinner, you won't recognize your need for a Savior. The Bible says we "all have sinned and fall short of the glory of God" (Romans 3:23).

Second, you have to *repent* of your sins. *Repentance* is an old English word that means you're willing to turn from your sin toward Jesus Christ; it literally means making a U-turn on the road of life—having a change of heart and a change of mind. It means being willing to follow Jesus and receive Him as your Savior and Lord. Jesus said, "Repent and believe the Good News!" (Mark 1:15).

Third, in order to demonstrate true belief, you have to be willing to *receive*. To truly receive, you have to trust in and depend fully on Jesus Christ, and Jesus Christ only, to be the Lord of your life here and now, your Savior for all eternity.

It takes more than *knowledge* (as the Bible tells us, even the devil knows about Jesus—and trembles). It takes more than *agreeing* that the knowledge we have is correct (the Bible tells us that even the devil agrees that Jesus is Lord). What it takes is putting *trust* in Jesus alone for eternal life. The requirements for eternal life aren't based on what *you can do*, but instead—don't miss this—on what *Jesus Christ has already done!* Jesus is ready and waiting to exchange His perfection for your imperfection.

According to Jesus Christ, those who *realize* they're sinners, *repent* of their sins, and *receive* Him as Savior and Lord are "born again" (John 3:3)— not physically, but spiritually. The reality of our salvation doesn't depend on our feelings, but rather on the promise of the Savior, who says to us: "I tell you the truth, whoever hears my word and believes him who sent me has eternal life and will not be condemned; he has crossed over from death to life" (John 5:24).

JOHN 3:16

*"For God so loved the world that he gave
his one and only Son, that whoever believes in him
shall not perish but have eternal life."*

For more information, see Hank Hanegraaff, "Does your relationship with God make you sure you will go to heaven when you die?" It is available through Christian Research Institute, www.equip.org. For further study, see John MacArthur, *Hard to Believe: The High Cost and Infinite Value of Following Jesus* (Nashville: Thomas Nelson Publishers, 2003).

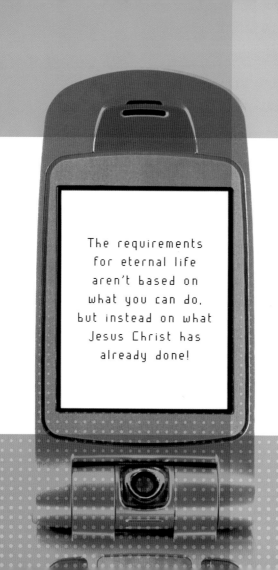

The requirements
for eternal life
aren't based on
what you can do,
but instead on what
Jesus Christ has
already done!

What Is Sin?

E ven though it's politically incorrect today to talk about sin, the Scriptures make it crystal clear that "all have sinned and fall short of the glory of God" (Romans 3:23).

But from a biblical perspective, what *is* sin?

First, sin isn't just murder, rape, or robbery. Sure, it's all of those things—but sin is also failing to do the things we should do, along with doing things that we shouldn't.

Simply put, *sin* is a word that describes anything that fails to meet God's standard of perfection. Therefore, sin is what stands between you and a satisfying relationship with God. Just as light and dark can't exist together, neither can God and sin coexist.

Second, sin is a barrier between us and other people. You only need to look online or listen to the evening news to see how true this really is. We live in an era when terrorism is a real and viable fear, an age when the world as we know it could be instantly obliterated by nuclear war.

Finally, sin is the deprivation of good. In this form, sin is characterized by a *lack of something* rather than being something itself.

1 JOHN 3:4–6

"Everyone who sins breaks the law; in fact, sin is lawlessness. But you know that he appeared so that he might take away our sins. And in him is no sin. No one who lives in him keeps on sinning. No one who continues to sin has either seen him or known him."

For further study, see Carl F. H. Henry's *Basic Christian Doctrines* (Grand Rapids: Baker Book House, 1962).

Sin is failing to do the things we should...
SINS OF OMISSION

Not forgiving (Matthew 6:15)

Failing to honor others (Romans 12:9)

Failing to keep your fervor (Romans 12:9)

Failing to serve or give (Romans 12:9)

Failing to live at peace (Romans 12:18)

Failing to love God (Deuteronomy 6:4; Mark 12:30)

Failing to love your neighbor as yourself (Mark 12:31)

Failing to trust God (Proverbs 3:5; Isaiah 26:4)

Failing to trust Christ (John 14:1)

Failing to worship God (Deuteronomy 6:13)

Failing to honor God (Proverbs 3:9; John 5:3)

Failing to honor the Son (John 5:23)

Failing to believe in Jesus (John 3:16–18; 6:29)

Failing to honor one's parents (Exodus 20:12)

Failing to give thanks to God (Psalm 105:1; Romans 1:21)

Failing to glorify God (Psalm 34:3; Romans 1:21)

Failing to fear the Lord (Deuteronomy 6:13; Proverbs 3:7)

Failing to test new teaching by Scripture (Acts 17:11; 1 Thessalonians 5:21)

Failing to discern and guard against false teachers and prophets (Matthew 7:15–20; Acts 20:28–31)

Failing to learn and believe Scripture (Deuteronomy 6:6; 2 Timothy 2:15)

Failing to guard life and doctrine (1 Timothy 4:16)

Failing to repay debts (Romans 13:7)

Failing to care for orphans and widows in distress (James 1:20)

Failing to defend the faith (1 Peter 3:15)

Failing to share the gospel (Matthew 28:19)

...and doing things we shouldn't.
SINS OF COMMISSION

Wrong teaching
(Matthew 23:15)

Insincere love (Romans 12:9)

Causing someone else to sin
(Mark 9:42)

Sexual impurity
(Romans 1:24)

Homosexuality
(Romans 1:26–27)

Idolatry (Romans 1:24)

Greed (Romans 1:29)

Blasphemy (Mark 3:29)

Misusing the Lord's name
(Exodus 20:7)

Selfish ambition
(Galatians 5:20)

Fits of rage (Galatians 5:20)

Slave trading (1 Timothy 1:10)

Lying (Exodus 23:1;
Revelation 21:8)

Hypocrisy (1 Peter 2:1)

Drunkenness
(1 Corinthians 6:10)

Stealing (Exodus 20:15;
1 Corinthians 6:10)

Sorcery (Deuteronomy 18:10)

Witchcraft
(Deuteronomy 18:10)

Divination
(Deuteronomy 18:10)

Interpreting omens
(Deuteronomy 18:10)

Consulting the dead
(Deuteronomy 18:11)

Astrology (Deuteronomy
18:9–13; Isaiah 47:13–14)

Depravity (Romans 1:29)

Envy (Romans 1:29;
1 Peter 2:1)

Deceit (Romans 1:29;
1 Peter 2:1)

Murder (Romans 1:29)

Strife (Romans 1:29)

Malice (Romans 1:29;
1 Peter 2:1)

Gossip (Romans 1:29)

Slander (Romans 1:30;
1 Peter 2:1)

Hating God (Romans 1:30)

Insolence (Romans 1:30)

Arrogance (Romans 1:30)

Boastfulness (Romans 1:30)

Inventing evil (Romans 1:30)

Disobeying parents
(Romans 1:30)

– 3 –

How Does the Bible Define Faith?

✳

The shield of faith described by the apostle Paul in his letter to the Ephesian Christians is hugely important because it's the grace "with which you can extinguish all the flaming arrows of the evil one" (Ephesians 6:16). This promise carries utter certainty, a divine assurance that faith equips us to escape the very extremities of evil.

But what is *faith*?

First, the Bible defines faith as "being sure of what we hope for and certain of what we do not see" (Hebrews 11:1). In biblical vernacular, faith is a *channel of living trust*—an assurance—that stretches from man to God. In other words, it's the *object* of faith that makes faith faithful.

Second, faith is the assurance that God's promises will never fail, even if we don't get to experience them in our lifetime. Hebrews 11 emphasizes that we trust God to fulfill His promises for the future (the unseen) based on what He has already fulfilled in the past. Therefore our faith isn't blind; it's based purely and unswervingly on God's proven faithfulness.

Finally, the faith that serves to protect us in spiritual warfare shouldn't be confused with mere knowledge. Millions worldwide believe in the trustworthiness of Billy Graham; they've heard him proclaim the Good News on television, yet they don't believe that his message is based on reality. Because of this, they possess the knowledge it takes to be saved, but they don't have saving faith.

Others hear the message and agree that it's real, but—due to the hardness of their hearts—still don't believe. Instead, like the demons, they continue living in fearful anticipation of the judgment to come (see James 2:19).

Some, however, have what Scripture describes as genuine, justifying faith—a faith that doesn't just know about the gospel and agree that its content corresponds to reality, but a faith through which they're transformed.

JOB 13:15
"Though he slay me, yet will I hope in him."

For further study, see Hank Hanegraaff, *The Covering: God's Plan to Protect You from Evil* (Nashville: W Publishing Group, 2002), chapter 7; and also *Christianity in Crisis* (Eugene, Ore.: Harvest House Publishers, 1993), part 2.

– 4 –

Can Christians Lose Their Salvation?

✳

Believers are sharply divided on this question. Some say Christians *can* lose their salvation, and as a result have to be born again if they "fall away." Others argue that true believers *can't* lose their salvation by sinning, but that they can apostatize, or walk away from their salvation. And still others believe that salvation begins at the moment of conversion (not death), and that it continues for all eternity. I hold this latter view, for several reasons.

First, outward appearances can be deceiving. Consider Judas. For three years, he was part of Christ's inner circle. As far as anyone could tell, he was a true follower of Jesus. Yet Jesus characterized Judas as "a devil" (John 6:70). The book of Hebrews warns us that there were Jews who, like Judas, tasted God's goodness and yet turned from His grace. They acknowledged Christ with their lips, but their apostasy proved their faith wasn't real.

Second, remember that the definition of everlasting life is exactly what it sounds like—"life everlasting." Our lives don't begin when we die; they begin when we embrace our Savior, who died in our place! In the same way that our physical birth can't be undone, our spiritual birth also can't be undone. Christ said, "Ye must be born again" (John 3:7 KJV), not "Ye must be born again…and again…and again." In Philippians, Paul praises God for the knowledge that "He who began a good work in you will carry it on to completion" (1:6).

The Bible is full of passages proving that believers are secure in their salvation. John 5:24 says that he who "believes…*has* eternal life" (emphasis added); 1 Corinthians 1:8 promises that Christ will "keep you strong to the end"; and Jude 1:24 guarantees that God "is able to keep you from falling and to present you before his glorious presence without fault."

Finally, Ephesians 1:13–14 offers us this certainty: "You were marked in him with a seal, the promised Holy Spirit, who is a deposit guaranteeing our inheritance until the redemption of those who are God's possession."

"My sheep listen to my voice;
I know them, and they follow me.
I give them eternal life, and they shall never perish;
no one can snatch them out of my hand.
My Father, who has given them to me, is greater
than all; no one can snatch them
out of my Father's hand."

For further study, see Hank Hanegraaff, "Safe and Secure," available from CRI at www.equip.org.

Our lives don't begin when we die;
they begin when we embrace
our Savior, who died in our place!

What Does It Mean to Say
the Holy Spirit Is *in* You?

Over the past several decades, I've been asked this "*in*" question in a variety of ways, such as: What does it mean to say God is "in" my life; Jesus is "in" my heart; or the Holy Spirit is "in" me? Does it mean that everyone simultaneously has a little piece of God in them? Or is the Bible communicating something far more precious?

First, saying that the Holy Spirit is *in* you isn't pointing out *where* the Holy Spirit is physically located, but rather acknowledging that you've come into an intimate, personal relationship with Him through faith and repentance. So the preposition "in" isn't a *locational*, but rather a *relational* term. And when Jesus says, "The Father is in me, and I in the Father" (John 10:38), He doesn't mean a physical location; He means the intimacy of friendship.

Just because the Holy Spirit isn't *spatially* locatable within us doesn't mean that He's not *actively* locatable within us. He works to conform us to the image of Christ, intensifying the intimacy of our relationship to God.

Finally, according to the Scriptures, the Holy Spirit isn't a physical being, so asking *where* the Holy Spirit is just confuses categories. Asking spatial questions about a Being who doesn't have extension in space makes about as much sense as asking what the color blue tastes like. King Solomon revealed how absurd it is to believe that the infinite Holy Spirit can be physically contained in any finite space, let alone the human body, when he said, "Will God really dwell on earth? The heavens, even the highest heaven, cannot contain you. How much less this temple I have built!" (1 Kings 8:27).

1 CORINTHIANS 6:19

"Do you not know that your body is
a temple of the Holy Spirit, who is in you,
whom you have received from God?"

For further study, see Hank Hanegraaff, "The Indwelling of the Holy Spirit," from CRI at www.equip.org.

– 6 –

How Important Is It for a Christian to Attend Church?

✳

From beginning to end, the Bible teaches us that our Christian life needs to be lived out within the context of the family of faith (Acts 2; Ephesians 3:4–15).

Simply put, the Bible doesn't encourage "Lone Ranger" Christians. You see, we're not born again as rugged individuals. Instead, we're born into a body of believers, and Christ is our head. Hebrews 10:25 tells us, "Let us not give up meeting *together*, as some are in the habit of doing" (emphasis added).

It's a simple fact that spiritual growth is impossible apart from membership in a healthy, well-balanced church. It is in the church that we receive the Word and sacraments as means of grace. And it is crucial that we mirror the example of the early Christians, who "devoted themselves to the apostles' teaching and to the fellowship, to the breaking of bread and to prayer" (Acts 2:42).

It's within the church that we worship together, experience fellowship, and learn how to witness.

But obviously, our church membership doesn't save us. As someone once said so well, walking into a church doesn't make you a Christian any more than walking into a garage makes you a car. The point is that we're rescued from God's wrath, forgiven of all our sins, and declared righteous before God solely by grace, through faith, on account of Jesus Christ (Romans 1:17; 3:21–4:0; Ephesians 2:8–9).

HEBREWS 10:25

"Let us not give up meeting together, as some are in the habit of doing, but let us encourage one another—and all the more as you see the Day approaching."

For further study, see Hank Hanegraaff, "How do I find a good church?" *The Bible Answer Book Volume 1* (Nashville: J. Countryman, 2004): 39–46.

How Do I Find a Good Church?

✳

One of the questions I'm most frequently
asked is, "How do I find a good church?"
This question has become even more
important in recent years because of the massive
impact televangelism has had on our culture. In all
too many cases, worship has been replaced by
entertainment, and fellowship has been transformed
into individualism. In view of these cultural shifts, it's
critical that Christians understand what comprises a
healthy, well-balanced church.

The first sign of a healthy, well-balanced church is
a pastor who is committed to leading the community
of faith in the *worship* of God through prayer, praise,
and proclamation. *Prayer* is so inextricably woven into
the fabric of worship that it would be unthinkable to
have a church service without it. From the very
beginning of the early Christian church, prayer has
been a primary means of worshiping God. Through
prayer, we have the privilege of expressing adoration
and thanksgiving to the One who saved us, sanctifies
us, and one day will glorify us. In fact, Jesus Himself

30 THE BIBLE ANSWER BOOK FOR STUDENTS

set the pattern by teaching His disciples the Prayer of Jesus (Matthew 6:9–13).

Praise is another key ingredient of worship. Scripture urges us to "speak to one another with psalms, hymns and spiritual songs" (Ephesians 5:19). Singing psalms is a magnificent way to intercede, instruct, and understand Scripture. In addition, the great hymns of the faith have stood the test of time and are rich in theological tradition and truth. Spiritual songs, in turn, communicate the freshness of our faith. So it's crucial that we respect our spiritual heritage by preserving contemporary compositions.

Along with prayer and praise, *proclamation* is key to vibrant worship. Paul urged his protégé Timothy to "preach the Word; be prepared in season and out of season; correct, rebuke and encourage— with great patience and careful instruction. For the time will come when men will not put up with sound doctrine. Instead, to suit their own desires, they will gather around them a great number of teachers to say what their itching ears want to hear" (2 Timothy 4:2–3). Church leaders must once again produce in their people a holy hunger for the Word of God. For it is through the proclamation of God's Word that believers are edified, exhorted, encouraged, and equipped.

Furthermore, a healthy, well-balanced church is evidenced through its *oneness*. Christ breaks the barriers of gender, race, and background and unites us as one under the banner of His love. Oneness is experienced through *community*, *confession*, and *contribution*.

Community is visible in baptism, which symbolizes our entrance into a body of believers who are one in Christ. It's a sign and a seal that we've been buried to our old life and raised to newness of life through His resurrection power. Communion is an expression of this. As we partake of the elements, we partake of what they symbolize—Christ, through whom we are one. Our fellowship on earth, celebrated through communion, is a foretaste of the heavenly fellowship we'll one day share when symbol gives way to substance.

A further expression of our oneness in Christ is our common *confession* of faith—a core set of beliefs, which have been rightly referred to as "essential Christianity." These beliefs, which have been codified in the creeds of the Christian church, form the basis of our unity as the body of Christ. The old maxim bears repeating: "In essentials, unity; in nonessentials, liberty; and in all things, clarity."

We also experience oneness through the *contribution* of our time, talents, and treasures.

The question we need to be asking isn't "What can the church do for me?" but "What can I do for the church?" Too often today when members of the body hurt, we send them to find help outside the church. That is exactly why the apostle Paul exhorts us to "share with God's people who are in need. Practice hospitality" (Romans 12:13).

Finally, a healthy, well-balanced church is one that is committed to equipping believers to be effective *witnesses* to what they believe, why they believe, and Who they believe. In the Great Commission, Christ called believers not to make mere converts, but to "make disciples" (Matthew 28:19). A disciple is a learner or follower of the Lord Jesus Christ.

We have to be prepared to communicate *what* we believe. In other words, we must be equipped to communicate the gospel. If Christians don't know how to share their faith, it's because they've never been through basic training. The gospel of Christ should become such a part of our vocabulary that sharing it is second nature.

We also need to be ready to share *why* we believe what we believe. As Peter puts it, we must "always be prepared to give an answer to everyone who asks you to give the *reason* for the hope that you have. But do this with gentleness and respect" (1 Peter 3:15, emphasis added). Too many today think that explaining the gospel clearly should be the job of scholars and theologians, but that's not true! Being able to defend your faith isn't an option; it is basic training for *every Christian.*

In addition to being prepared to communicate the what and why of our faith, we need to be prepared to communicate the *Who* of our faith. Every theological mistruth begins with a misconception of the nature of God. Thus, in a healthy, well-balanced church, believers are trained to communicate glorious doctrines of the faith such as the Trinity and the deity of Jesus Christ. It is crucial that we, like the early Christian church, understand the biblical concept of the priesthood of all believers. It isn't the pastor's calling to do the work of ministry single-handedly. Rather, the pastor is called "to prepare God's people for works of service, so that the body of Christ may be built up until we all reach unity in the faith and in the knowledge of the Son of God and become mature" (Ephesians 4:12–13).

In summary, you'll know that you've found a good church if God is *worshiped* in Spirit and in truth through prayer, praise, and the proclamation of the Word; if the *oneness* the church shares in Christ is tangibly manifested through community, confession, and contribution; and if the church is equipping its members as *witnesses* who can communicate what they believe, why they believe, and Who they believe.

ACTS 2:42
"They [followers of Christ] devoted themselves to the apostles' teaching and to the fellowship, to the breaking of bread and to prayer."

For further study see Hank Hanegraaff, "How to Find a Healthy Church," available from CRI at www.equip.org.

– 8 –

Should Christians Judge Their Leaders' Teachings?

❋

The answer to this question may surprise you. Not only is judging permissible; it is our Christian *responsibility*.

The reason for this is because nobody's teachings are above sound judgment—especially those of influential leaders! The Bible tells us that authority and accountability go hand in hand (cf. Luke 12:48). The greater the responsibility one holds, the greater the need for accountability (cf. James 3:1).

First, the precedent for making right judgments comes from Scripture itself. In the Old Testament, the Israelites were commanded to practice sound judgment by thoroughly testing the teachings of their leaders (Deuteronomy 13). Similarly, in the New Testament, the apostle Paul commands the Thessalonians to test all things and to "hold fast to that which is good" (1 Thessalonians 5:21 NASB). In fact, Paul even praised the Bereans for testing his teachings (Act 17:11).

Jesus cautioned His followers not to judge self-righteously (Mathew 7:1–5), but He also counseled them to make judgments based on right standards (John 7:24). Just look at Jesus' often-misquoted command, "Do not judge, or you too will be judged"—Jesus then encourages His followers to judge false prophets, whose teachings and example lead people astray (Matthew 7:15–20). Through this, we can see that He commands us not to judge hypocritically, but that nonetheless we're called to make judgment.

Finally, common sense alone should alert us to how important it is to declare public *and* private judgments regarding false doctrine. During the infamous Tylenol scare in 1982, for example, public warnings were issued by the media and the medical community regarding the physical danger of ingesting Tylenol capsules that someone had laced with cyanide. In the same way, when spiritual cyanide is spreading through the Christian community, we're obligated to warn others. A biblical example of this happened when Paul publicly rebuked Hymenaeus and Philetus, whose teachings "spread like gangrene" (2 Timothy 2:17–18; cf. Galatians 2:11–14).

JOHN 7:24

*"Stop judging by mere appearances,
and make a right judgment."*

For further study, see Hank Hanegraaff, "The Untouchables: Are 'God's Anointed' Beyond Criticism?" and Bob and Gretchen Passantino, "Christians Criticizing Christians: Can It Be Biblical?" both available through the Christian Research Institute (CRI) at www.equip.org.

The greater the
responsibility
one holds, the greater
the need for
accountability.

– 9 –

What Does It Mean to Interpret the Bible Literally?

✳

For more than a decade, popular TV personality Bill Maher has made his living ridiculing Christianity. Maher has gone so far as to tell his TV audience that the Bible was "written in parables. It's the idiots today who take it literally."

Even a cursory reading shows us that Scripture is a treasury filled with a wide variety of literary styles ranging from poetry, proverbs, and psalms to historical narratives, didactic epistles, and apocalyptic revelations. To say that the Bible was written in parables and that those who read it *literally* must be "idiots" is at best a form of fundamentalism and at worst a serious misunderstanding of biblical interpretation. In order to read the Bible for all it's worth, we need to interpret it just like we would other forms of communication—in its most obvious and natural sense. As such, we must read it as literature, paying close attention to *form*, *figurative language*, and *fantasy imagery*.

First, in order to interpret the Bible literally, we have to pay special attention to what is known as form or genre. In other words, to interpret the Bible as literature, it's crucial that we carefully consider the kind of literature we're interpreting. A legal document is very different from a prophetic oracle; in the same way, there's a big difference in genre between Leviticus and Revelation. This is particularly important when considering writings that are difficult to categorize, like Genesis, which is largely a historical narrative interlaced with symbolism and repetitive poetic structure.

If Genesis were reduced to an allegory filled with abstract ideas about temptation, sin, and redemption without any connection to actual historical events, the very foundation of Christianity would be destroyed. If the historical Adam and Eve didn't eat the forbidden fruit and descend into a life of habitual sin that resulted in death, then there's no need for redemption. On the other hand, if we consider Satan to be an actual slithering snake, we not only misunderstand the nature of fallen angels, but we might also suppose that Jesus triumphed over the work of the devil by stepping on the head of a serpent (Genesis 3:15) rather than through His work on the cross (Colossians 2:15).

But sometimes a literal interpretation does as much damage to the text as a spiritual interpretation that empties it of objective meaning. The "literal at all costs" method of interpreting is particularly dangerous when it comes to books of the Bible where imagery is central. For example, in Revelation the apostle John sees a vision of an angel swinging a sharp sickle and gathering grapes into "the great winepress of the wrath of God." According to Scripture, the blood flowing from the winepress rises as high as "the horse bridles, by the space of a thousand and six hundred furlongs" (Revelation 14:19–20 KJV). Interpreting this kind of apocalyptic imagery in a wooden, literal sense would be ridiculous.

Furthermore, it's crucial to see that Scripture—particularly apocalyptic portions—is filled with figurative language, which differs greatly from literal language (where words mean exactly what they say). Figurative language requires readers to use their imagination in order to understand what the author is getting at. Such imaginative leaps are the rule rather than the exception; virtually every genre of literature contains metaphorical language. We might even say that figurative language is the main way that God communicates spiritual realities to His children. In other words, God communicates spiritual realities through earthly, observed events, persons, or objects—things that are probably best described as "living metaphors."

A metaphor is a comparison that equates a word or phrase with something it doesn't literally represent. Far from minimizing biblical truths, metaphors serve as magnifying glasses that show us truths we might otherwise miss. This creates meaning that lies beyond woodenly literal interpretations, and requires the use of your imagination to grasp the meaning. For example, when Jesus said, "I am the bread of life" (John 6:48), it's obvious that He wasn't saying He was literally physical bread; rather, He was metaphorically saying that He's the essence of true life.

Biblical metaphors should never be seen as empty opportunities for subjective flights of fantasy. On the contrary, biblical metaphors are always objectively meaningful, authoritative, and true.

Hyperbole is another figure of speech found often in prophetic passages. In essence, hyperbole uses exaggeration for effect or to make a point. If you step onto a scale and exclaim, "Oh my goodness, I weigh a ton!" it's obvious that you don't mean you literally weigh two thousand pounds. Similarly, when an NBA commentator looks up at the clock, sees a minute left, and says, "There's a world of time left in this game," he's using hyperbole to say that in the NBA, a lot can happen in sixty seconds.

Hyperbole is everywhere in the Bible. This is especially true of prophetic passages. Isaiah used hyperbole when he predicted judgment on Babylon: "See the day of the LORD is coming—a cruel day, with wrath and fierce anger—to make the land desolate and destroy the sinners within it. *The stars of heaven and their constellations will not show their light. The rising sun will be darkened and the moon will not give its light*" (Isaiah 13:9–10, emphasis added). To those unfamiliar with biblical language, these words might well be taken to mean that the end of the world was at hand. In reality, Isaiah was prophesying that the Medes were about to put an end to the glories of the Babylonian empire.

The preceding verses are packed with prophetic hyperbole: "Wail, for the day of the LORD is near; it will come like destruction from the Almighty. Because of this, *all hands will go limp, every man's heart will melt*. Terror will seize them, pain and anguish will grip them; they will writhe like a woman in labor. They will look aghast at each other, *their faces aflame*" (vv. 6–8, emphasis added). Even the most literal interpreter knows that Isaiah isn't inferring that all hands will literally go limp and that every heart will literally melt. Nor is he literalistically predicting that every Babylonian face will be on fire, any more than John is using wooden literalism to prophesy that the two witnesses in Revelation will emit flames of fire from their mouths (Revelation 11:5).

Finally, it's important to correctly interpret fantasy imagery in apocalyptic passages—such as an enormous red dragon with seven heads and ten horns (Revelation 12:3); locusts with human faces, women's hair, and lions' teeth (9:7); and a beast that resembled a leopard, but with feet like a bear and a mouth like a lion (13:2). What is distinct about such fantasy images is that they don't correspond to anything in the real world. But while fantasy images are unreal, they provide a real way to think about reality.

Fantasy imagery, of course, is fraught with danger. That danger, however, doesn't lie in its use, but in its abuse. In Revelation 12, the apostle John describes "an enormous red dragon with seven heads and ten horns and seven crowns on his heads. His tail swept a third of the stars out of the sky and flung them to the earth" (vv. 3–4). Many Christians abuse such imagery by interpreting it in a woodenly literalistic fashion, and they miss the whole point of the passage. Not only would a single star—let alone a third of the stars—obliterate the earth, but dragons are the stuff of mythology, not theology. Thus, the danger with fantasy imagery lies in equating those images with unbiblical notions.

While the Scriptures should be read as literature, we have to remember that the Bible is far more than a work of great literature. The Scriptures are uniquely inspired by the Spirit. As Peter puts it, "No prophecy of Scripture came about by the prophet's own interpretation. For prophecy never had its origin in the will of man, but men spoke from God as they were carried along by the Spirit" (2 Peter 1:20–21). We must pray that the Spirit, who inspired the Scriptures, illumines our minds to what is *in* the text.

2 TIMOTHY 2:15
"Do your best to present yourself to God as one approved, a workman who does not need to be ashamed and who correctly handles the word of truth."

For further study, see Hank Hanegraaff, *The Apocalypse Code* (Nashville: W Publishing Group, 2007).

Scripture—particularly apocalyptic portions— is filled with figurative language, which differs greatly from literal language.

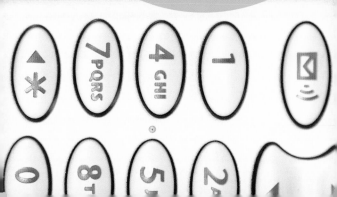

What Is Apologetics?

As we move into what has been referred to often as "post-Christian America," it's increasingly important for Christians to know what they believe, as well as *why* they believe it. The apostle Peter puts it this way: "*Always* be prepared to give an answer *[apologia]* to everyone who asks you to give the reason for the hope that you have. But do this with gentleness and respect" (1 Peter 3:15, emphasis added).

First, apologetics is the defense of the faith "once for all entrusted to the saints" (Jude 3). The word *apologetics* comes from the Greek word *apologia*, which means "a reasoned defense." It means providing an *answer*, not an *apology* in today's sense of the word. Just like good attorneys defend their clients in the courtroom by presenting solid evidence and sound reasoning, apologists defend the truth of Christianity through well-reasoned answers in response to skeptics and seekers.

Furthermore, apologetics is *pre-evangelism*; it is the handmaiden to evangelism. It's using our logical answers as opportunities to share the good news of the gospel. The Christian faith isn't a blind faith, but rather a faith firmly rooted in history and evidence.

Finally, apologetics is *post-evangelism*. In the midst of all the doubt and despair that threaten to submerge our faith, it's important to familiarize ourselves with the pillars of our faith: that God created the universe; that Jesus Christ demonstrated He is God through the immutable fact of His resurrection; and that the Bible is divine, not just human, in origin. In a nutshell, this is what apologetics is all about.

If you're looking for a truly rewarding experience, think about becoming an apologist. Not only will you experience the power and presence of the Holy Spirit working through you, but you may just find yourself in the middle of an angelic praise gathering when you've helped a lost son or daughter of Adam find his or her way into the kingdom of God.

COLOSSIANS 4:5–6
"Be wise in the way you act toward outsiders; make the most of every opportunity. Let your conversation be always full of grace, seasoned with salt, so that you may know how to answer everyone."

For further study, see William Lane Craig, *Reasonable Faith* (Wheaton, IL: Crossway, 1994).

11

How Many Explanations Are There for the Existence of Our Universe?

hilosophical naturalism—the worldview behind evolutionism—can provide only three explanations.

First, that the universe is merely an illusion. This idea carries little weight in an age of scientific enlightenment.

Second, that the universe sprang from nothing. This proposition flies in the face of both the laws of cause and effect and energy conservation. As has been well said, "Nothing comes from nothing, nothing ever could." Or, to put it another way, there simply are no free lunches. The conditions that hold true in this universe prevent any possibility of matter springing out of nothing.

Third, that the universe has existed forever. The law of entropy, which predicts that a universe that has eternally existed would have died an "eternity ago" of heat loss, devastates this hypothesis.

There is, however, one other possibility. It is found in the first chapter of the first book of the

Bible: "In the beginning God created the heavens and the earth." In an age of empirical science, nothing could be more certain, clear, or correct.

ROMANS 1:20

"For since the creation of the world God's invisible qualities—his eternal power and divine nature—have been clearly seen, being understood from what has been made, so that men are without excuse."

For further study, see James W. Sire, *The Universe Next Door: A Basic Worldview Catalog*, 3rd ed. (Downers Grove, Ill.: InterVarsity Press, 1997); C. S. Lewis, *Mere Christianity* (New York: Macmillan, 1952).

12

If We Can't See God,
How Can We Know He Exists?

✳

t isn't uncommon to hear skeptics call Christians "irrational" for believing in a God they can't see. In reality, it's irrational for such skeptics to suppose that what can't be seen doesn't exist.

First, the fact that something can't be seen doesn't mean it does not exist. We know that black holes, electrons, the laws of logic, and the law of gravity exist despite the fact that we can't see them. Even a full-blown empiricist believes in the law of gravity while standing atop the Eiffel Tower!

Further, as King David wrote, "The heavens declare the glory of God; the skies proclaim the work of his hands" (Psalm 19:1). Or in the words of the apostle Paul, "God's invisible qualities—his eternal power and divine nature—have been clearly seen, being understood from what has been made, so that men are without excuse" (Romans 1:20). To put it another way, the order and complexity of the visible, physical universe undoubtedly testify to the existence of an uncaused first cause.

Finally, God can be seen through the Person and work of Jesus Christ. As Paul explains, "In Christ all the fullness of the Deity lives in bodily form" (Colossians 2:9). Indeed, the incarnation of Jesus Christ is the supreme act of God's self-revelation. Through the ministry of the Holy Spirit, we experience the power and presence of God in a way that is more real than even the physical world we live in.

1 CORINTHIANS 13:12
"Now we see but a poor reflection
as in a mirror; then we shall see face to face.
Now I know in part; then I shall know
fully, even as I am fully known."

For further study, see J. P. Moreland and William Lane Craig, *Philosophical Foundations for a Christian Worldview* (Downers Grove, IL: InterVarsity Press, 2003); see also Lee Strobel, *The Case for a Creator* (Grand Rapids: Zondervan, 2004).

13

Who Made God?

Naturalism is a philosophy arguing that 1) the universe is merely an illusion, 2) the universe sprang from nothing, and 3) the universe eternally existed. As you can see, none of these views explains the existence of the universe. Logically, we can turn only to the possibility that "God created the heavens and the earth" (Genesis 1:1).

However, it does bring up this question: Who made God?

First, unlike the universe, which, according to modern science had a beginning, God is *infinite* and *eternal*. And as an infinite and eternal being, God can reasonably be called the uncaused First Cause.

Second, we reach a logical dead end if we suppose that because the universe had a cause, the cause of the universe must have had a cause. Here's why: an infinite regression of finite causes doesn't answer the question of *source*; it only makes the *effects* more numerous.

Third, simple logic dictates that the universe isn't just an illusion. It didn't spring out of nothing

(nothing comes from nothing; nothing ever could), and it hasn't existed for eternity (the law of entropy predicts that a universe that has existed eternally would have died an "eternity ago" of heat loss).

Thus, the only philosophically reasonable possibility remaining is that the universe was made by an unmade Cause greater than itself.

PSALM 90:2

"Before the mountains were born or you brought forth the earth and the world, from everlasting to everlasting you are God."

For further study, see Paul Copan, *That's Just Your Interpretation: Responding to Skeptics Who Challenge Your Faith* (Grand Rapids: Baker Books, 2001), 69–73.

– 1 4 –

What Makes Christianity the One True Religion?

❋

Christianity is unique among the religions of the world for several reasons. First, unlike other religions, Christianity is rooted in history and evidence. Jesus of Nazareth was born in Bethlehem in Judea during the reign of Caesar Augustus and was put to death by Pontius Pilate, a first-century Roman governor. The testimony of His life, death, and resurrection is validated both by credible eyewitness testimony and by credible extra-biblical evidence. No other religion can legitimately claim this kind of support from history and evidence.

Furthermore, of all the influential religious leaders of the world (a list that includes Buddha, Moses, Zoroaster, Krishna, Lao Tzu, Muhammad, and Baha'u'llah), only Jesus claimed to be God in human flesh (Mark 14:62). And His wasn't an empty boast. For through the historically verifiable fact of resurrection, Christ vindicated His claim to deity (Romans 1:4; 1 Corinthians 15:3–8). Other religions, such as Buddhism and Islam, claim miracles in support of their faith; however, unlike Christianity, all of these miracles lack historical evidence.

Finally, Christianity is unique because it follows a logical belief pattern. Some Christian doctrines may be beyond our powers of understanding, but unlike the claims of other religions, they are never irrational or contradictory.

Christianity is also unique in that it clearly accounts for the incredible phenomena we encounter in everyday life: the human mind, laws of science, laws of logic, ethical norms, justice, love, meaning of life, problem of evil and suffering, and truth. In other words, Christianity corresponds with the reality of our present condition.

2 PETER 1:16
"We did not follow cleverly invented stories when we told you about the power and coming of our Lord Jesus Christ, but we were eyewitnesses of his majesty."

For further study, see James W. Sire, *The Universe Next Door*, 3rd ed. (Downers Grove, Ill.: InterVarsity Press, 1997); and Lee Strobel, *The Case for Christ* (Grand Rapids: Zondervan Publishing House, 1998).

How Do We Know That the Bible Is Divine Rather than Human in Origin?

✳

T o defend our faith, we have to be prepared to demonstrate that the Bible is divine, rather than human, in origin. When we can successfully accomplish this, we can answer a host of other objections by appealing to Scripture.

To begin with, the Bible has stronger manuscript support than any other work of classical history— including Homer, Plato, Aristotle, Caesar, and Tacitus. Just as amazing is the fact that the Bible has been virtually unaltered since the original writing, which is attested to by scholars who have compared the earliest extant manuscripts with manuscripts written centuries later. Additionally, the reliability of the Bible is affirmed by the testimony of its authors, who were eyewitnesses—or close associates of eyewitnesses—to the recorded events, and by secular historians who confirm the many events, people, places, and customs chronicled in Scripture.

Furthermore, archaeology is a powerful witness to the accuracy of New Testament documents. Over and over, comprehensive archaeological fieldwork and careful biblical interpretation affirm the Bible's reliability. For example, recent archaeological finds support biblical details surrounding the trial that led to Jesus' torment—including Pontius Pilate, who ordered Christ's crucifixion, as well as Caiaphas, the high priest who presided over the religious trials of Christ. It is telling when secular scholars must review their biblical criticisms in light of solid archaeological evidence.

Finally, the Bible records predictions of events that couldn't be known or predicted by chance or common sense. For example, the book of Daniel (written before 530 BC) accurately predicts the progression of kingdoms from Babylon through the Medo-Persian Empire, the Greek Empire, and then the Roman Empire, ending with the persecution and suffering of the Jews under Antiochus IV epiphanies with his desecration of the temple, his untimely death, and freedom for the Jews under Judas Maccabeus (165 BC). It is statistically ridiculous that any or all of the Bible's specific, detailed prophecies could have been fulfilled through chance, good guessing, or deliberate deceit.

2 Timothy 3:16

*"All Scripture is God-breathed
and is useful for teaching, rebuking, correcting
and training in righteousness."*

For further study, see Lee Strobel, *The Case for Christ: A Journalist's Personal Investigation of the Evidence for Jesus* (Grand Rapids: Zondervan, 1998).

It is statistically
ridiculous that any or all
of the Bible's specific,
detailed prophecies could
have been fulfilled
through chance,
good guessing,
or deliberate deceit.

16

Don't All Religions Lead to God?

B efore I answer this question, a word of warning: Anyone who answers no may be called narrow-minded and intolerant. That said, my answer is, "No, not all religions lead to God, and it is incorrect and illogical to maintain that they do."

First, when you begin to examine world religions such as Judaism, Hinduism, and Buddhism, you'll immediately recognize that they directly contradict one another. For example, Moses taught that there was only one God; Krishna believed in many gods; and Buddha was agnostic. Logically, they can all be wrong but they can't all be right.

Furthermore, the road of religion leads steeply uphill, while the road of Christianity descends downward. To put it another way, religion is fallen humanity's attempt to reach up and become acceptable to God through what we do; Christianity, on the other hand, is a divine gift based on what Christ has *done*. He lived the perfect life that we could never live and offers us His perfection as an absolutely free gift.

Finally, Jesus taught that there was only one way to God. "I am *the way* and *the truth* and *the life*," said Jesus. "No one comes to the Father except through me" (John 14:6, emphasis added). Moreover, Jesus validated His claim through the immutable fact of His resurrection. The opinions of all other religious leaders are equally valid in that they're equally worthless. They died and are still dead. Only Jesus had the power to lay down His life and take it up again, so His opinion is infinitely more valid than theirs.

ACTS 4:12

"Salvation is found in no one else,
for there is no other name under heaven given
to men by which we must be saved."

For further study, see John MacArthur, *Why One Way? Defending an Exclusive Claim in an Inclusive World* (Nashville: W Publishing Group, 2002); and Ronald Nash, *Is Jesus the Only Savior?* (Grand Rapids: Zondervan, 1994).

17

What Happens to a Person
Who Has Never Heard of Jesus?

✳

One of the most frequently asked questions on the *Bible Answer Man* broadcast is "What happens to those who have never heard of Jesus?" Will God condemn people to hell for not believing in someone they've never heard of?

First, people aren't condemned to hell for not believing in Jesus. Rather, they're *already* condemned because of their *sin*. So the real question isn't "How can God send someone to hell?" It's "How can God condescend to save any one of us?"

Furthermore, if ignorance were a ticket to heaven, the greatest evangelistic enterprise wouldn't be a Billy Graham crusade but instead a cover-up campaign that would focus on ending evangelism, burning Bibles, and closing churches. Soon no one will have heard of Christ and everyone will be on their way to heaven.

Finally, it should be emphasized that everyone has the light of both creation and conscience. God isn't fickle! If we respond to the light we have, God will give us more light. In the words of the apostle Paul: "From one man he made every nation of men, that they should inhabit the whole earth; and he determined the times set for them and the exact places where they should live. God did this so that men would seek him and perhaps reach out for him and find him, though he is not far from each one of us" (Acts 17:26–27).

JOHN 14:6

*"I am the way and the truth and the life.
No one comes to the Father except through me."*

For further study, see Ronald H. Nash, *Is Jesus the Only Savior?* (Grand Rapids: Zondervan, 1994). See also Hank Hanegraaff, "Is Jesus the Only Way?" available through the Christian Research Institute (CRI) at www.equip.org.

18

How Were People Who Lived Before the Time of Christ Saved?

✳

Some say that people who lived before Christ were saved by keeping the Law. The Scriptures, however, tell us something else.

First, the Bible from beginning to end shows that the saved throughout history come to faith in exactly the same way—*by grace alone through faith alone on account of Christ alone.* The apostle Paul quotes the Old Testament extensively to drive home the reality that no one has been, or ever will be, declared righteous by observing the Law (Romans 3:20).

Furthermore, Paul points to Abraham, the father of the Jews, to prove that salvations come through faith, not works that we perform. In his words, "If, in fact, Abraham was justified by works, he had something to boast about—but not before God. What does the Scripture say? 'Abraham believed God, and it was credited to him as righteousness'" (Romans 4:2–3; see also Genesis 15:6 and Galatians 3:6–9).

Finally, Jesus Christ is the substance that fulfills the prophecies in Old Testament (Luke 24:44;

Romans 3:21–22; Hebrews 1:1–3). Each year the Jews celebrated the Passover to keep them focused on the One who was to come to die for their sin (1 Corinthians 5:7; Hebrews 11:28, 39–40). As Hebrews says, "The law is only a shadow of the good things that are coming—not the realities themselves" (10:1).

Jesus Christ stands at the apex of history. Just like people today look back in history to Christ's sacrifice on the cross, so did people who lived before the time of Christ look forward to His sacrifice for them.

"What then shall we say that Abraham,
our forefather, discovered in this matter?
If, in fact, Abraham was justified by works, he had
something to boast about—but not before God.
What does the Scripture say? 'Abraham believed God,
and it was credited to him as righteousness.'
Now when a man works, his wages are not credited
to him as a gift, but as an obligation.
However, to the man who does not work but
trusts God who justifies the wicked, his faith is
credited as righteousness. David says the same thing
when he speaks of the blessedness of the man to whom
God credits righteousness apart from works:
'Blessed are they whose transgressions are forgiven,
whose sins are covered. Blessed is the man whose sin
the Lord will never count against him.'
Is this blessedness only for the circumcised, or also for
the uncircumcised? We have been saying that
Abraham's faith was credited to him as righteousness.
Under what circumstances was it credited?
Was it after he was circumcised, or before?
It was not after, but before!"

For further study, see Bruce Milne, *Know the Truth* (Downer's Grove:
InterVarsity Press, 1998), 189–91.

Jesus Christ
stands at the apex
of history.

– 19 –

Why Does God Allow Bad Things to Happen to Good People?

✳

T his is probably the most common question Christian celebrities are asked on shows like *Larry King Live*. And from people's responses, it might seem like there are as many answers to that question as there are religions!

But in reality, there are only three basic answers: pantheism, philosophical naturalism, and theism. Pantheism denies the existence of good and evil, because in this view god is all and all is god. Philosophical naturalism (the worldview that encourages evolutionism) says that everything is a function of random processes and there is no such thing as good or evil. Theism alone has a relevant response—and only Christian theism can answer the question satisfactorily.

First, Christian theism acknowledges that God created the potential for evil, because God created humans with the freedom of choice. We choose to love or hate, do evil or good. The record of history bears eloquent testimony to the fact that humans of their own free will have actualized the reality of evil through such choices.

Furthermore, without choice, love is meaningless. God is neither a cosmic rapist who forces His love on people, nor a cosmic puppeteer who forces people to love Him. Instead, God, the personification of love, grants us the freedom of choice. Without such freedom, we would be little more than preprogrammed robots.

Finally, the fact that God created the potential for evil by granting us freedom of choice ultimately will lead to the best of all possible worlds—a world in which "there will be no more death or mourning or crying or pain" (Revelation 21:4). Those who choose Christ will be redeemed from evil by His goodness and will forever be able *not* to sin.

ROMANS 8:28
*"We know that in all things God works
for the good of those who love him, who have been
called according to his purpose."*

For further study, see Joni Eareckson Tada and Steven Estes, *When God Weeps* (Grand Rapids: Zondervan, 1997); and Lee Strobel, *The Case for Faith* (Grand Rapids: Zondervan, 2000), chapter 1.

–20–

If Christianity Is True, Why Are So Many Atrocities Committed in the Name of Christ?

✸

T his is a classic smokescreen question often asked to avoid having to wrestle with the evidence for authentic Christianity. At best, it involves a hasty generalization. At worst, it's a way of "poisoning the well."

To begin with, this question was anticipated by Christ, who long ago proclaimed that His followers would be recognized by the way they lived their lives (John 15:8). So to classify people who are responsible for instigating atrocities as Christian is to beg the question of who Christ's disciples are to begin with. As Jesus pointed out, not everyone who calls Him "Lord" is the real deal (Matthew 7:21–23).

Furthermore, this question implies that Christianity must be false on the basis that atrocities have been committed in Christ's name. There's no reason, however, that we can't turn the argument around and claim that Christianity must be true because so much good has been done in the name of Christ.

Think of the countless hospitals, schools, universities, and relief programs that have been instituted as a direct result of people who have the sacred name of Christ upon their lips.

Finally, those who use this argument fail to realize that the validity of Christianity doesn't rest on sinful men but rather on the perfection of Jesus Christ alone (Hebrews 7:26; 1 Peter 2:22). Moreover, the fact that professing Christians commit sins only serves to prove the premise of Christianity—namely, "all have sinned and fall short of the glory of God" (Romans 3:23); thus, all are in need of a Savior (1 John 3:4–5).

MATTHEW 7:21–23

"Not everyone who says to me,
'Lord, Lord,' will enter the kingdom of heaven,
but only he who does the will of my Father who is in
heaven. Many will say to me on that day,
'Lord, Lord, did we not prophesy in your name,
and in your name drive out demons and
perform many miracles?' Then I will tell them plainly,
'I never knew you. Away from me, you evildoers!'"

For further study, see R. C. Sproul, *Reason to Believe* (Grand Rapids: Zondervan, 1982); Lee Strobel, *The Case for Faith* (Grand Rapids: Zondervan, 2000), chapters 4 and 7.

– 21 –

What Is Truth?

***

This is the same question Pontius Pilate asked Jesus. In the greatest irony in history, Pilate stood toe-to-toe with the personification of Truth—and yet missed its reality. Postmodern thinkers are in the same position that Pilate was. They stare at truth but fail to recognize it.

First, truth is an aspect of the nature of God Himself. In other words, to put on truth is to put on Christ, for Christ is "truth" (John 14:6) and Christians are to be the bearers of truth. As writer Os Guinness explains, Christianity isn't true simply because it works (pragmatism). It isn't true because it feels right (subjectivism). It isn't true because it's someone's opinion (relativism). No, it's true because it's anchored in the Person of Christ.

Furthermore, truth is anything that corresponds to reality. Truth doesn't yield to the size and strength of the latest lobby group. Truth isn't a matter of preference or opinion. Rather, truth is true even if everyone denies it, just as a lie is a lie even if everyone affirms it.

Finally, truth is essential to a realistic worldview. When sophistry, sensationalism, and superstition attack truth, our view of reality becomes seriously skewed. The death of truth spells the death of civilization. However, as Aleksandr Solzhenitsyn once said, "One word of truth outweighs the entire world."

JOHN 18:37–38

"'You are a king, then!' said Pilate.
Jesus answered, 'You are right in saying I am a king.
In fact, for this reason I was born, and for
this I came into the world, to testify to the truth.
Everyone on the side of truth listens to me.'
'What is truth?' Pilate asked."

For further study, see Os Guinness, *Time for Truth* (Grand Rapids: Baker Books, 2000).

Should Christians Be Tolerant?

✳

T he word *tolerance* has come to mean "all views are equally valid and all lifestyles equally appropriate." Because of this, the belief that Jesus is the only way is often seen as *in*tolerant. Rather than bowing to culture, Christians need to know how to expose the flaws in today's definition of tolerance, while simultaneously exemplifying *true* tolerance.

First, saying that all views are equally valid *sounds* tolerant, but in reality it's a contradiction in terms. You see, if all views are equally valid, then the Christian view must be valid; however, the Christian view holds that not all views are equally valid. So the redefinition of tolerance in our culture is a self-refuting proposition.

Even more to the point, we don't tolerate people with whom we agree; we tolerate people with whom we *disagree*. If all views were equally valid, there would be no need for tolerance!

Today's redefinition of tolerance is especially dangerous because it doesn't leave room for objective moral judgment. A modern terrorist could be deemed as virtuous as a Mother Teresa. With no enduring reference point, society's values are being reduced to matters of preference—and that's often based upon the mere opinions of celebrities! Our moral basis for resolving international disputes and condemning such obviously evil practices as genocide, oppression of women, and child prostitution is being seriously compromised.

Christians must reject today's tolerance and revive *true* tolerance. True tolerance holds the notion that, despite our differences, we treat every person we meet with the dignity and respect due them as those created in the image of God.

True tolerance doesn't say we can't proclaim the truth, but it does encourage doing so with gentleness and with respect (cf. 1 Peter 3:15–16). In a world that's becoming increasingly intolerant of Christianity, Christians have to show tolerance without sacrificing truth. When it comes to personal relationships, tolerance is a virtue; but when it comes to truth, it's a travesty.

JUDE 1:22-23

*"Be merciful to those who doubt;
snatch others from the fire and save them;
to others show mercy, mixed with fear—hating even
the clothing stained by corrupted flesh."*

For further study, see Paul Copan, *"True for You, but Not for Me": Deflating
the Slogans That Leave Christians Speechless* (Minneapolis: Bethany House
Publishers, 1998); see also Josh McDowell and Bob Hostetler, *The New
Tolerance* (Wheaton, Ill.: Tyndale House Publishers, 1998).

True tolerance holds
the notion that, despite
our differences,
we treat every person
we meet with the dignity
and respect due
them as those created
in the image of God.

23

Is the Big Bang Biblical?

✳

The Big Bang claims that the universe began billions of years ago as an infinitely dense point called a "singularity," and that it's been expanding ever since. Though the Big Bang isn't taught in the Bible, the theory does lend scientific support to the scriptural truth that God created the universe *ex nihilo* (out of nothing).

First, like the Bible, the Big Bang suggests that the universe had a beginning, so it stands in stark opposition to the scientifically silly suggestion that the universe eternally existed, not to the biblical account of origins.

Second, if the universe had a beginning, it also had to have a cause. According to empirical science, whatever begins to exist "must have a cause equal to or greater than itself." So the Big Bang flies in the face of the philosophically ridiculous idea that the universe sprang from nothing apart from an uncaused First Cause.

Finally, even though evolutionists support Big Bang cosmology, the Big Bang itself doesn't entail biological evolution. In other words, the Big Bang theory answers questions about the origin of the space-time universe, *not* questions concerning the origin of biological life on earth.

We shouldn't ever stake our faith on Big Bang cosmology. However, we *can* be absolutely confident that as human understanding of the universe continues to grow, it will ultimately point to the One who spoke the universe into existence.

PSALM 19:1
"The heavens declare the glory of God;
the skies proclaim the work of his hands."

For further study, see Paul Copan and William Lane Craig, *Creation Out of Nothing: A Biblical, Philosophical, and Scientific Exploration* (Grand Rapids: Baker Academic, 2004): 17–19; see also J. P. Moreland, *Scaling the Secular City: A Defense of Christianity* (Grand Rapids: Baker Book House, 1987): 33–34, and Lee Strobel, *The Case for a Creator* (Grand Rapids: Zondervan, 2004), especially chapter 5.

24

How Can We Be Sure
That Evolution Is a Myth?

✳

D r. Louis Bounoure, former director of
research at the French National Center
for Scientific Research, calls evolution "a
fairy tale for grown-ups." I call it a cruel hoax! In
fact, the arguments that support evolutionary
theory are incredibly weak.

First, the fossil record is an embarrassment to
evolutionists. No verifiable transitions from one
kind to another have been found. Charles Darwin
had an excuse; in his day, fossil finds were relatively
scarce. Today, however, we have plenty of fossils—
yet we haven't found even one legitimate transition
from one kind to another.

Furthermore, in Darwin's day such complex
structures as a human egg were thought to be quite
simple—for all practical purposes, little more than
a microscopic blob of gelatin. Today, we know that
a fertilized human egg is among the most organized,
complex structures in the universe. In an age of
scientific enlightenment, it's incredible that people

are willing to maintain that something so complex happened by chance. Like an egg or the human eye, the universe is a masterpiece of precision and design that couldn't have come into existence by chance.

Finally, while chance is a blow to the theory of evolution, the laws of science are a bullet to its head. The basic laws of science, including the laws of *effects and their causes*—*energy conservation* and *entropy*—strengthen the creation model for origins and weaken the evolutionary hypothesis. While I would fight for a person's right to have faith in science fiction, we must resist evolutionists who attempt to brainwash people into thinking that evolution is science.

PSALM 19:1–4

"The heavens declare the glory of God;
the skies proclaim the work of his hands.
Day after day they pour forth speech;
night after night they display knowledge.
There is no speech or language
Where their voice is not heard.
Their voice goes out into all the earth,
Their words to the ends of the world."

For further study, see Hank Hanegraaff, *Fatal Flaws: What Evolutionists Don't Want You to Know* (Nashville: W Publishing, 2003); Phillip E. Johnson, *Darwin on Trial*, 2nd ed. (Downers Grove, Ill.: InterVarsity Press, 1993).

Did Darwin Have a Deathbed Conversion?

In order to demonstrate the falseness of evolution, Bible-believing Christians for more than a century have passed on the story of Charles Darwin's deathbed conversion. Evolutionists have attempted to counter them by loudly protesting that Darwin died believing that Christianity was a fraud and that chance was the creator.

In response, it should first be noted that whether Darwin did or didn't renounce evolution *doesn't* speak to the issue of whether evolution is true or false. Maybe Darwin renounced evolution because he was senile or he had taken a mind-altering drug. He may have even just hedged his bets with some "eternal fire insurance."

As followers of the One who proclaimed Himself to be not only "the way" and "the life" but also "the truth" (John 14:6), we have to set the standard for the evolutionist, *not* vice versa. James Fegan was correct when he described the Darwin legend as "an illustration of the recklessness with which the

Protestant Controversialists seek to support any cause they are advocating."

In *The Darwin Legend*, James Moore painstakingly documents the fact that there is *no* substantial evidence that Darwin ever repented, but there is abundant evidence that he consistently held to his evolutionary paradigm.

EXODUS 20:16
"You shall not give false testimony against your neighbor."

For further study, see James Moore, *The Darwin Legend* (Grand Rapids: Baker Books, 1994).

– 26 –

If Jealousy Is a Sin, How Can God Be Jealous?

✳

T he second of the Ten Commandments explicitly tells us that God is a jealous God (Exodus 20:4–5; cf. 34:14), yet in Galatians Paul condemns jealousy in the same breath as idolatry (5:19–20). How can this be?

First, there is such a thing as sanctified jealousy. For example, jealousy is the proper response of a husband or wife whose trust has been violated through infidelity. Whenever an exclusive covenant relationship is dishonored, sanctified jealousy is the passionate zeal that fights to restore that holy union. The jealousy of God for His holy name and for the exclusive worship of His holy people is sanctified.

And there is also such a thing as sinful jealousy. In this sense, jealousy is painfully coveting another's advantages. The apostle Paul lists jealousy as an act of the sinful nature. He says, "The acts of the sinful nature are obvious: sexual immorality, impurity and debauchery; idolatry and witchcraft; hatred, discord, *jealousy*, fits of rage, selfish ambition, dissensions,

factions and envy; drunkenness, orgies, and the like"
(Galatians 5:19–21, emphasis added).

God personifies sanctified jealousy, and those
who reflect His character must be zealous for the
things of God. The Bible is full of heroes like Elijah
(1 Kings 19:10, 14), David (Psalm 69:9), and Paul
(2 Corinthians 11:2) whose jealousy for God's glory
motivated self-sacrifice and radical reform. The
quintessential example, however, is found in the
incarnate Christ who exercised the epitome of
sanctified jealousy by overturning the tables of the
moneychangers in the temple—a symbolic gesture
condemning the Jewish leaders of His day for
dishonoring God through their contemptible
religiosity (Matthew 21:12–13; John 2:17; cf.
Jeremiah 7:9–15).

2 CORINTHIANS 11:2
*"I am jealous for you with a godly jealousy.
I promised you to one husband, to Christ, so that I
might present you as a pure virgin to him."*

For further study, see J. I. Packer, *Knowing God* (Downers Grove, Ill.:
InterVarsity Press, 1982), 151–58.

– 27 –

Does God Know the Future?

specific group of Christians called "open theists" are currently saying that God doesn't have perfect knowledge of the future. How do we respond to this as Christians?

First, the Bible from beginning to end demonstrates the omniscience of God. In the words of Isaiah, God knows "the end from the beginning" (Isaiah 46:10). God's knowledge is exhaustive, and it includes the future (cf. Job 37:16; Psalm 139:1–6; 147:5; Hebrews 4:12–13).

Furthermore, if God's knowledge of the future were fallible, biblical predictions that depend on human agency might have turned out wrong. Even Jesus' predictions in the Olivet Discourse could have failed, undermining His claim to deity. God Himself could have failed the biblical test for a prophet (Deuteronomy 18:22). Indeed, if God's knowledge of the future weren't complete, we would be foolish to trust Him to answer our prayers. This would undo the "confidence we have in approaching God: that if we ask anything according to his will, he hears

88   THE BIBLE ANSWER BOOK FOR STUDENTS

us. And if we know that he hears us—whatever we ask—we know that we have what we asked of him" (1 John 5:14–15).

Open theists say that God can't know the future exhaustively because He changes His plans as a result of what people do. But in reality, it isn't God who changes; *people change in relationship to God.*

As an analogy, think about walking directly into a headwind—you struggle against it, but if you make a U-turn you find the wind at your back. It isn't the wind that has changed; you have changed in relationship to the wind. In the same way, God's promise to destroy Nineveh wasn't aborted because He didn't know the future but because the Ninevites, who had walked in opposition to God, turned from their wicked ways.

All of God's promises to bless or judge need to be viewed in light of the condition that God withholds blessing on account of disobedience and withholds judgment on account of repentance (Ezekiel 18; Jeremiah 18:7–10).

"Remember the former things, those of long ago;
I am God, and there is no other; I am God,
and there is none like me. I make known the end
from the beginning, from ancient times,
what is still to come. I say: My purpose will stand,
and I will do all that I please."

For further study, see "Does God Repent?" in Hank Hanegraaff, *The Bible
Answer Book: Volume 2* (Nashville: J. Countryman, 2006), 70.

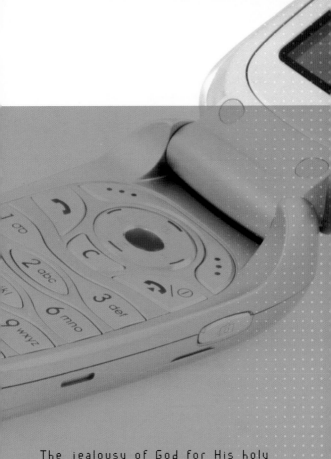

The jealousy of God for His holy name and for the exclusive worship of His holy people is sanctified.

– 2 8 –

What Does It Mean to Say That God Is Omnipresent?

✳

T he Bible clearly portrays God's omnipresence. But what exactly does that mean? Is God dispersed throughout the universe? Or does omnipresence refer to God's nearness to all of creation all the time?

First, when Scripture speaks of God as omnipresent or present everywhere (Psalm 139), it isn't communicating that He is physically distributed throughout the universe, but that He is simultaneously present (with all His fullness) to every part of creation. Thus, Scripture is talking about God's creative and sustaining relationship to the cosmos rather than His physical location in the cosmos.

Furthermore, to speak of God's omnipresence in terms of His physical location in the world rather than His relationship to the world has more in common with the panentheism of heretical process theology (currently popular in liberal circles) than with classical Christian theism. Panentheism holds that God is intrinsically "in" the world (like a hand in a glove), while classical theism holds that God properly exists outside of time and space (Isaiah 57:15).

Finally, the danger of speaking about God in locational terms is that it logically implies He's a material being by nature. The apostle John clearly tells us, "God is Spirit, and his worshipers must worship in spirit and in truth" (John 4:24).

PSALM 139:7–10

"Where can I go from your Spirit?
Where can I flee from your presence?
If I go up to the heavens, you are there;
if I make my bed in the depths, you are there.
If I rise on the wings of the dawn,
if I settle on the far side of the sea,
even there your hand will guide me,
your right hand will hold me fast."

For further study, see Gordon R. Lewis, "Attributes of God," in Walter A. Elwell, ed., *Evangelical Dictionary of Theology*, 2nd ed. (Grand Rapids: Baker Academic, 2001), 492–99.

– 29 –

Does God Have a Gender?

✳

It has become pretty popular in Christian circles to use "politically correct" language when referring to God. Some even supplement the Trinitarian language of Father, Son, and Holy Spirit with feminine formulations like Mother, Child, and Womb. This raises an important question: Does God have a gender?

First, the Bible tells us that "God created man in his own image, in the image of God he created him; male and female he created them" (Genesis 1:27). As God created both male and female in His image, He doesn't participate in one or the other gender; rather, He transcends gender.

Furthermore, while the Bible uses masculine titles for God, such as Father and Son, it also employs feminine images of God, such as mother (Isaiah 49:14–15; 66:13) and midwife (Isaiah 66:9). Likewise, His judgment of Israel is likened to that of a mother bear robbed of her cubs (Hosea 13:8).

Whether masculine or feminine, all such images are anthropomorphisms (human metaphors) or

94 THE BIBLE ANSWER BOOK FOR STUDENTS

personifications (abstract metaphors) that reveal God to us in ways we can understand.

The language we use for God needs to clarify, not confuse. Where the Bible doesn't call for it, we should refrain from tampering with traditional titles for God. It would be a big mistake to sacrifice the nature of God on the altar of political correctness.

GALATIANS 3:28–29

"There is neither Jew nor Greek, slave nor free, male nor female, for you are all one in Christ Jesus. If you belong to Christ, then you are Abraham's seed, and heirs according to the promise."

For further study, see Leslie Zeigler, "Christianity or Feminism?" in William A. Dembeski and Jay Wesley Richards (eds.), *Unapologetic Apologetics* (Downers Grove, Ill.: InterVarsity Press, 2001), 179–86.

30

Did Jesus Claim to Be God?

T hen Jesus came to Caesarea Philippi, He asked His disciples the mother of all questions: *"Who do you say I am?"* (Matthew 16:15; Mark 8:29; Luke 9:20). Mormons answer this question by saying that Jesus is the spirit brother of Lucifer; Jehovah's Witnesses answer by saying that Jesus is the archangel Michael; New Agers say Jesus is an avatar or enlightened messenger. Jesus, however, answered by claiming that He was God.

First, Jesus claimed to be the unique Son of God. As a result, the Jewish leaders tried to kill Him because in "calling God His own Father, [Jesus was] making Himself equal with God" (John 5:18 NASB). In John 8:58, Jesus went so far as to use the very words by which God revealed Himself to Moses from the burning bush (Exodus 3:14). To the Jews, this was the height of blasphemy! They knew that in doing this, Jesus was clearly claiming to be God.

On yet another occasion, Jesus explicitly told the Jews, "'I and the Father are one.' Again the Jews picked up stones to stone him, but Jesus said to them, 'I have shown you many great miracles from the Father. For which of these do you stone me?' 'We are not stoning you for any of these,' replied the Jews, 'but for blasphemy, because you, a mere man, claim to be God'" (John 10:30–33).

Furthermore, Jesus made an unmistakable claim to deity before the chief priests and the whole Sanhedrin. Caiaphas the high priest asked him: "'Are you the Christ, the Son of the Blessed One?' 'I am,' said Jesus. 'And you will see the Son of Man sitting at the right hand of the Mighty One and coming on the clouds of heaven'" (Mark 14:61–62).

A person unfamiliar with the Bible might miss Jesus' words here. However, Caiaphas and the council did not. They knew that in saying He was "the Son of Man" who would come *on the clouds of heaven,* Jesus was making an open reference to the "son of man" in Daniel's prophecy (Daniel 7:13–14). And in doing so, Jesus wasn't just claiming to be the preexistent Sovereign of the universe; He was also prophesying that He would vindicate His claim by judging the very court that was now condemning Him.

Even more important is the fact that by combining Daniel's prophecy with David's proclamation in Psalm 110, Jesus was effectively claiming that He would sit upon the throne of

Israel's God and share God's glory. To students of the Old Testament, this was the height of blasphemy. Thus, "they all condemned him as worthy of death" (Mark 14:64).

Finally, Jesus claimed to possess the very attributes of God. For example, He claimed *omniscience* by telling Peter, "This very night, before the rooster crows, you will disown me three times (Matthew 26:34). He declared *omnipotence* by resurrecting not only Lazarus from the dead (John 11:43) but also Himself (see John 2:19). And He professed *omnipresence* by promising He would be with His disciples "to the very end of the age" (Matthew 28:20).

Jesus also said to the paralytic in Luke 5:20, "Friend, your sins are forgiven." By doing this, He claimed a right reserved for God alone. And when Thomas worshiped Jesus, saying, "My Lord and my God!" (John 20:28), Jesus responded with commendation, not condemnation.

REVELATION 1:17–18

"I am the First and the Last. I am the Living One; I was dead, and behold I am alive for ever and ever!"

For further study, see Millard J. Erickson, *The Word Became Flesh: A Contemporary Incarnational Christology* (Grand Rapids: Baker Book House, 1996).

Jesus claimed
to possess the very
attributes of God.

31

If God Can't Be Tempted, How Was Jesus Tempted?

✳

O n one hand, Scripture tells us that "God cannot be tempted by evil" (James 1:13). On the other, it says that during His wilderness sojourn, Jesus was tempted by the evil one (Matthew 4:1–11). So could Jesus be tempted, or couldn't He?

First, for sin to take place, there must be a sinful inner response to sinful suggestion. Though Satan appealed to Jesus' natural human desires (e.g., hunger), our Lord didn't fantasize over Satan's suggestion. To mull over Satan's suggestion even for a moment would have constituted sin. And if Jesus had sinned, He couldn't have been our Savior.

Furthermore, even though Jesus didn't have any sinful tendencies that led Him toward evil, Satan's temptations were still as real as the flesh on His bones. Even those who are born into sin can identify with being tempted to do something they aren't drawn to do. As an analogy, most mothers would never consider killing their children—even if offered a life free from suffering. Nonetheless, the natural desire to avoid suffering would make such a temptation real.

Finally, in saying "God cannot be tempted by evil," James focuses on God as the self-sufficient Sovereign of the universe—a Being with no unmet needs at all. On the other hand, the stories about Jesus' temptation focus on God-Incarnate who experienced all the physical and psychological needs known by humanity—hunger, fatigue, and a desire for self-preservation. Through this contrast, we can see that the biblical truths that God can't be tempted and yet Christ *was* tempted are complementary, not contradictory.

HEBREWS 4:15

"For we do not have a high priest
who is unable to sympathize with our weaknesses,
but we have one who has been tempted
in every way, just as we are—yet was without sin."

For further study, see Adam Pelser, "Genuine Temptation and the Character of Christ," *Christian Research Journal* 30, 3 (2007), available through the Christian Research Institute (CRI) at www.equip.org.

How Can We Be Sure about the Resurrection of Christ?

✳

I f devotees of the kingdom of the cults, adherents of world religions, or liberal scholars are correct, the biblical account of the resurrection of Christ is either fiction, fantasy, or a huge fraud. But on the other hand, if Christianity is factually reliable His resurrection is the greatest feat in human history. No middle ground exists. The Resurrection is either history or hoax, miracle or myth, fact or fantasy.

First, liberal and conservative scholars alike agree that the body of Jesus was buried in the private tomb of Joseph of Arimathea. As a member of the Jewish court that condemned Jesus, Joseph of Arimathea isn't likely to be Christian fiction (Mark 15:43); Jesus' burial in the tomb of Joseph of Arimathea is substantiated by Mark's Gospel (15:46) and therefore is far too early to have been the subject of legendary corruption; the earliest Jewish response to the resurrection of Christ presupposes the empty tomb (Matthew 28:11–13); and in the centuries that followed the Resurrection, the story of the empty tomb was spread by Jesus' friends and foes alike.

Additionally, when you understand the role of women in first-century Jewish society, what's extraordinary is that this empty tomb story would feature females as the discoverers of the empty tomb. The fact that women are the first witnesses to the empty tomb is most reasonably explained by the reality that—like it or not—they were the discoverers of the empty tomb. This shows that the Gospel writers faithfully recorded what happened, even if it was embarrassing. In short, early Christianity couldn't have survived an identifiable tomb containing the corpse of Christ.

Furthermore, Jesus gave His disciples many convincing proofs that He had risen from the dead. Paul, for example, points out that Christ "appeared to more than five hundred of the brothers at the same time, most of whom are still living, though some have fallen asleep" (1 Corinthians 15:6). It would have been one thing to attribute these supernatural experiences to people who had already died. It was quite another to attribute them to multitudes who were still alive. As the famed New Testament scholar of Cambridge University C. H. Dodd points out, "There can hardly be any purpose in mentioning the fact that most of the five hundred are still alive, unless Paul is saying, in effect, 'The witnesses are there to be questioned.'"

Finally, what happened as a result of the Resurrection is unprecedented in human history. In the span of a few hundred years, a small band of seemingly insignificant believers succeeded in turning an entire empire upside down. While it's conceivable that they would've faced torture, vilification, and even cruel deaths for what they fervently believed to be true, it's inconceivable that they would have been willing to die for what they knew was a lie. As Dr. Simon Greenleaf, the famous royal professor of law at Harvard puts it: "It if were not morally permissible for them to have been deceived in this matter, every human motive operated to lead them to discover and avow their error.... If then their testimony was not true, there was no possible motive for this fabrication."

"If there is no resurrection of the dead,
then not even Christ has been raised. And if Christ
has not been raised, our preaching is useless
and so is your faith. More than that, we are then
found to be false witnesses about God, for we
have testified about God that he raised Christ from
the dead. But he did not raise him if in fact the dead
are not raised. For if the dead are not raised,
then Christ has not been raised either. And if Christ
has not been raised, your faith is futile; you are
still in your sins. Then those also who have fallen
asleep in Christ are lost. If only for this life we have
hope in Christ, we are to be pitied more than
all men. But Christ has indeed been raised from the
dead, the firstfruits of those who have fallen asleep."

For further study, see Hank Hanegraaff, *The Third Day* (Nashville: W Publishing Group, 2003); Lee Strobel, *The Case for Christ* (Zondervan, 1999); and see especially William Lane Craig, *Reasonable Faith* (Crossway Books, 1996), chapter 8.

— 33 —

Was Jesus Really in the Grave for Three Days and Three Nights?

✳

esus specifically tells us, "As Jonah was three days and three nights in the belly of a huge fish, so the Son of Man will be three days and three nights in the heart of the earth" (Matthew 12:40). The Gospels also tell us that Jesus died on the day before the Sabbath (Friday) and rose on the day after the Sabbath (Sunday). How do we resolve this apparent contradiction?

First, in Jewish idiom, any part of a day counted as a day-night unit. So there's no need to literalistically demand that seventy-two hours be accounted for. This is particularly evident in light of Jesus' own contention that He would rise *on* the third day, not *after* the third day and night had ended (Matthew 16:21; 17:23; 20:19; Luke 24:46; cf. Matthew 26:61; 27:40, 63–64).

Furthermore, the Gospels all declare that Jesus died on the Day of Preparation—Friday, the day leading up to the beginning of the Sabbath at sundown (Matthew 27:62; Mark 15:42; Luke

23:54; John 19:31, 42). The Gospel writers also show similar agreement regarding the discovery of Jesus' resurrection early in the morning on the day following the Sabbath—Sunday, the first day of the week (Matthew 28:1; Mark 16:1; Luke 24:1; John 20:1). So for people to suggest that Jesus died on Thursday and rose on Sunday contradicts the testimony of all four Gospel writers.

Finally, once knowledge of ancient culturally informed modes of oral and literary expression replaces a naive literalistic interpretation, the harmony of Scripture shines through. Jesus' sacrificial death and miraculous resurrection on the third day is the glorious archetypal fulfillment of Old Testament types, including the Passover Lamb (Exodus 12; cf. 1 Corinthians 5:7), Jonah's preservation for "three days and three nights" (Jonah 1:17), and the restoration of Israel "on the third day" that Hosea prophesied about (Hosea 6:2).

LUKE 24:46
"He told them, 'This is what is written:
The Christ will suffer and
rise from the dead on the third day.'"

For further study, see Hank Hanegraaff, *Resurrection* (Nashville: Word Publishing, 2000).

— 34 —

Why Pray if God
Already Knows What We Need?

✳

As a father of nine, I can tell you that I sometimes know what my children need before they ask. However, what I as an earthly father only sometimes know, our eternal Father always knows. This leads us to the question: If God knows what we need before we even ask, why bother asking at all?

First, it's crucial to recognize that supplication shouldn't be seen as the sum and substance of our prayers. Far from being just a way to present our daily requests to God, prayer is all about pursuing a dynamic relationship with Him.

Furthermore, God ordains not only the ends but the means. So to ask, "Why pray if God already knows what we need?" is like asking, "Why get dressed in the morning and go to class?" That's really no different than saying, "If God is going to do what He's going to do anyway, why bother doing anything at all?"

God has told us in Scripture that the work we do and the prayers we utter both produce results.

The fact that God knows the future doesn't mean that our futures are fatalistically determined any more than our knowing the sun will rise *causes* the sun to rise.

Finally, while our heavenly Father knows what we need before we even ask, it's through prayer that we grow utterly dependent on Him. And that alone is reason enough to pray without ceasing.

MATTHEW 6:7–8

"And when you pray, do not keep on babbling like pagans, for they think they will be heard because of their many words. Do not be like them, for your Father knows what you need before you ask him."

For further study, see Hank Hanegraaf, *The Prayer of Jesus: Secrets to Real Intimacy with God* (Nashville: W Publishing Group, 2001).

Do I Have to Forgive People
Who Refuse Forgiveness?

※

Jesus taught His disciples to pray, "Forgive us our debts, as we also have forgiven our debtors" (Matthew 6:12). Does that mean we have to forgive someone even if they refuse to reconcile?

First, the debts we owe one another are small change compared to the infinite debt we owe our heavenly Father. Because we've been forgiven an infinite debt, it's a horrendous evil to even consider withholding forgiveness from those who seek it. We always need to practice the kind of love that is *willing* to forgive those who wrong us.

Furthermore, forgiveness is by definition a two-way street leading to the restoration of fellowship. It requires someone who is *willing* to forgive, and someone who *wants* to be forgiven. If you are to forgive me, I must be repentant; otherwise, there can be no restoration of fellowship (i.e., forgiveness).

Finally, we must never suppose that our standard of forgiveness is higher than God's standard. He *objectively* offers us forgiveness and the restoration of fellowship. His forgiveness is not *subjectively* realized, however, until we repent (Luke 6:37–38).

MATTHEW 5:23–24

*"Therefore, if you are offering your gift
at the altar and there remember that your brother
has something against you, leave your gift
there in front of the altar. First go
and be reconciled to your brother; then come
and offer your gift."*

For further study, see Hank Hanegraaff, *The Prayer of Jesus: Secrets to Real Intimacy with God* (Nashville: W Publishing Group, 2001).

36

Is Tithing Relevant for Christians Today?

✳

If all the questions I'm asked to answer, this is beyond a doubt the most difficult. It's not only because the subject of tithing is hotly debated, but because I have to confess that I personally haven't always been faithful in giving a tenth or more to the work of the Lord. And I'm not alone in this—research shows that the majority of Christians not only don't tithe regularly; many actually give little or nothing at all. Therefore, while talking about this question is incredibly convicting, it is also increasingly important.

Randy Alcorn puts it well: tithing should be regarded as the training wheels of giving. Tithing is as important today as it has ever been. We all need to learn what it means to walk freely in Christian stewardship. In learning to give, we're also learning to lean more heavily upon our heavenly Father and less upon ourselves. Those who've traveled the Calvary road for any length of time know that God is ever faithful. Not only that, but as we weekly set aside our tithes and offerings we're reminded that all we are, or ever hope to be, is a gift from God.

Furthermore, as Moses communicated to the children of Israel, we tithe "so that [we] may learn to revere the Lord [our] God always" (Deuteronomy 14:23). As we all know, learning to reverence the name of God is a timeless principle—as crucial today as in the days of Moses. Long *before* Moses, the Bible records Jacob's promise to God: "Of all that you give me I will give you a tenth" (Genesis 28:22). Long *after* Moses, Jesus reaffirmed the practice of tithing (Matthew 23:23)—not for outward appearances, but as an outward expression of an inward reality.

Additionally, in the fourth century the great church father Jerome echoed the words of Malachi, who implied that failing to pay tithes and offerings was tantamount to "robbing" God—and that's a prescription for financial ruin (Malachi 3:8).

Finally, tithing in the Old Testament not only prepared God's people to become givers but produced a temple of great splendor. The Israelites, who pined for the pleasures and protection of pagan Egypt more than for the One who had miraculously parted the Red Sea, were transformed into joyful givers. The Bible chronicles the prayer of David as he thanked God for the very privilege of being able to give to the work of the Lord: "But who am I, and who are my people, that we should be able to give as generously as this? Everything comes from you, and we have given you only what comes from your hand…. And now I have seen with joy how willingly your people who are here have given to you" (1 Chronicles 29:14, 17).

What began as a spiritual discipline became pure delight. Really, there's no telling what can be accomplished in our generation if we, too, catch the joy of contagious giving. Not only would we spread the gospel around the globe, but we would be able to feed the hungry, clothe the naked, and care for the sick. Like our forefathers who founded great centers of Christian education, established countless hospitals, and funded relief organizations, we might also leave an indelible mark on our generation. But it's only when the training wheels of tithing come off that the world of free-will giving becomes our playground.

PROVERBS 3:9–10

"Honor the LORD with your wealth,
with the firstfruits of all your crops; then your barns
will be filled to overflowing, and your vats
will brim over with new wine."

For further study, see Randy Alcorn, *Money Possessions and Eternity*, rev.
ed. (Wheaton, Ill.: Tyndale House Publishers, 2003).

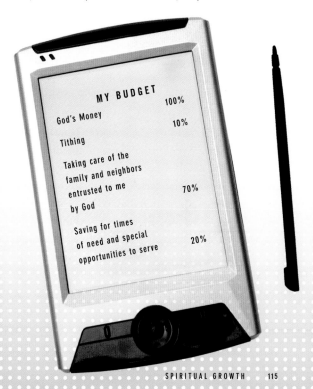

37

What Does the Bible Say about Wealth?

I'm convinced that the Bible teaches a form of Christian capitalism—in other words, responsibility associated with wealth. It doesn't promote making money for the sake of having money, but instead encourages us to use money for the kingdom. In other words, a biblical view of wealth involves an eternal perspective.

First, it's important we recognize that "the earth is the LORD's and everything in it, the world, and all who live in it" (Psalm 24:1). God is the Landlord; we are just tenants. We don't arrive with anything, and we won't take anything with us when we leave. Just remembering this can save us from a world of hurt.

Furthermore, poverty doesn't equal goodness, nor do riches mean righteousness. God prospers some, and He places others in more humble circumstances. If there were a one-to-one ratio between godliness and wealth, the godliest people in the world would be the wealthiest. A quick glance at *Forbes'* 100 Wealthiest People (in 2007, all billionaires for the first time in history) shatters this illusion.

Finally, it's important to view wealth with eternity in mind. In other words, lead your life here below as a responsible steward—whether you have a little or a lot—so that one day, at the judgment, God Himself will richly reward you (Matthew 25:21). It's your bank statement in *heaven* that counts (Matthew 6:19–21); if you fix your hope on the one you have down here, you're bankrupt no matter how many digits are next to your name.

MATTHEW 6:24
"No one can serve two masters.
Either he will hate the one and love the other,
or he will be devoted to the one and despise the other.
You cannot serve both God and Money."

For further study, see John Piper, *Desiring God: Meditations of a Christian Hedonist* (Sisters, Ore.: Multnomah Publishers, 1986), chapter 7. And see Hank Hanegraaff, *Christianity in Crisis* (Eugene, Ore.: Harvest House Publishers, 1993), part 5.

What Does the Bible Teach about Debt?

✳

Most Americans are drowning in debt, so much that our dependence on it begs the question: What does the Bible say about debt?

First, the Bible warns that "the borrower is servant to the lender" (Proverbs 22:7). As such, we're warned against the foolishness of being greatly indebted to anyone who may be unforgiving in his demand for repayment. We should seriously consider the wisdom of this proverb: "Do not be a man who strikes hands in pledge or puts up security for debts; if you lack the means to pay, your very bed will be snatched from under you" (Proverbs 22:26–27).

Furthermore, Scripture calls the failure to repay debts "wicked." In the words of the psalmist, "The wicked borrow and do not repay, but the righteous give generously" (Psalm 37:21). Likewise, the apostle Paul encourages believers to be diligent about repaying their debts (Romans 13:8).

Finally, whether in the theocracy of ancient Israel or the democracy of modern America, God's people are called to be good stewards of the resources that He has entrusted them with. If we lend to others, we should do so with kindness, and if we borrow, we should do so with prudence.

ROMANS 13:8

"Let no debt remain outstanding,
except the continuing debt to love one another, for he
who loves his fellowman has fulfilled the law."

Should Christians Celebrate Christmas?

✴

E very year around Christmastime, serious concerns are raised about whether—or to what extent—to celebrate Christmas. Some people argue that the origins of Christmas are pagan, others say that the Bible calls Christmas trees idolatrous, and still others suggest that Santa Claus is a dangerous fairy tale.

Let me start by saying that when Christmas was originally instituted, December 25 was indeed a pagan festival commemorating the birthday of a false god. While this is historical fact, what's frequently overlooked is that the church's choice of December 25 was intentional. Instead of Christianizing a pagan festival, the church established a rival celebration. Today, while the world has all but forgotten the Greco-Roman gods of antiquity, they're reminded every year that two thousand years ago Christ invaded time and space.

Furthermore, the Bible *doesn't* condemn Christmas trees as idolatrous. The passage being referred to, Jeremiah 10:2–4, could at first glance appear compelling, but in this case context precludes pretext. Jeremiah's description of a tree cut out of the forest, adorned with silver and gold and fastened with a hammer and nails so it won't totter, is a reference to wooden idols, not Christmas trees. Actually, Christmas trees originated in Christian Germany two thousand years after Jeremiah's condemnation of manmade idols! They evolved over time from two Christian traditions. One was a "paradise tree" hung with apples as a reminder of the Tree of Life in the Garden of Eden; the other was a triangular shelf holding Christmas figurines and decorated with a star. In the sixteenth century, these two symbols merged into the present Christmas tree tradition. Next Christmas, consider using the Christmas tree in the home of an unbeliever as an opportunity to explain the reason for the season, from the Fall to redemption in Christ.

Finally, far from being a dangerous fairy tale, "Santa Claus" is actually an Anglicized form of the Dutch name *Sinter Klaas*, which in turn is a reference to Saint Nicholas. According to tradition, Saint Nick not only lavished gifts on needy children but also supported the doctrine of the Trinity at the Council of Nicea in AD 325. Thus, Christians can look to Saint Nick as a genuine hero of the faith.

This December 25, as you celebrate the coming of Christ with a Christmas tree surrounded by presents, may the selflessness of Saint Nick be a reminder of the Savior who gave the greatest gift of all: "Greater love has no one than this, that he lay down his life for his friends" (John 15:13).

LUKE 2:8–14

"And there were shepherds living out in the
fields nearby, keeping watch over their flocks at night.
An angel of the Lord appeared to them,
and the glory of the Lord shone around them,
and they were terrified. But the angel said
to them, 'Do not be afraid. I bring you good news
of great joy that will be for all the people.
Today in the town of David a Savior has been
born to you; he is Christ the Lord. This will be a sign
to you: You will find a baby wrapped in cloths
and lying in a manger.' Suddenly a great company of
the heavenly host appeared with the angel,
praising God and saying, 'Glory to God
in the highest, and on earth peace to men
on whom his favor rests.'"

For further study, see Paul Maier, *The First Christmas* (Grand Rapids: Kregel Publications, 2001).

As you celebrate the coming
of Christ with a Christmas tree
surrounded by presents,
may the selflessness
of Saint Nick be a reminder
of the Savior who
gave the greatest gift of all:
"Greater love has no one
than this, that he lay
down his life for his friends"
(John 15:13).

How Should Christians Respond to Halloween?

✴

Many questions surround the October holiday of Halloween: Should we participate? Offer an alternative? Or ignore Halloween altogether? To answer these questions, it's helpful to look at Halloween from the perspective of history.

First, you should know that Halloween is rooted in the ancient Celtic feast of *Samhain* (sah-ween). The Druids believed that on the eve of Samhain, the veil between the present world and the world beyond was pierced, releasing demons, witches, and hobgoblins to harass the living. In order to make themselves immune from attack, people disguised themselves as witches, devils, and ghouls; attempted to ward off evil spirits by carving grotesque faces on gourds illuminated with candles; and placated the spirits with a variety of treats.

We can learn a lot by how the early Christians responded to Halloween. October 31, the eve prior to All Saints' Day, was designated as a spiritually edifying holiday (literally, "holy day") on which to proclaim the supremacy of the gospel over the superstition of ghosts. Thus, "All Hallows' Eve," from which the word *Halloween* is derived, was an attempt on the part of Christianity to overwhelm the tradition of ghouls with the truth of the gospel.

Finally, although Halloween is once again predominantly pagan, there is a silver lining. Like our forefathers, we can choose to celebrate All Hallows' Eve by focusing on heroes of the faith—those who, like Martin Luther, were willing to stand for truth no matter what the cost.

In the end, the "trick" is to treat Halloween as a strategic opportunity, not a time of satanic oppression.

HEBREWS 12:1

"Therefore, since we are surrounded by such a great cloud of witnesses, let us throw off everything that hinders and the sin that so easily entangles, and let us run with perseverance the race marked out for us."

See also Hank Hanegraaff, "Halloween: Oppression or Opportunity?" available from CRI, www.equip.org.

Can Christians Be Demonized?

Over the years, I've read a great many stories claiming that Christians can be demonized. In the end, they all have one thing in common: they overestimate the power and province of Satan. Some deliverance ministers make a greater attempt than others to provide biblical basis for the argument that a Christian can be inhabited by a demon. Inevitably, however, Scripture itself undermines their stories.

First, Christ Himself said it was impossible that a Christian could be inhabited by demons. Using the illustration of a house, Jesus asked, "How can anyone enter a strong man's house and carry off his possessions unless he first ties up the strong man?" (Matthew 12:29). In the case of a demon-possessed person, the strong man is obviously the devil. In a Spirit-indwelt believer, however, the strong man is God! The force of Christ's argument leads straight to the conclusion that, in order for demons to possess believers, they would first have to bind the One who occupies them—God Himself.

I found an equally airtight argument against Christian demonization in the Gospel of John. The Jews were once again accusing Jesus of being demon-possessed. Rather than avoid their accusations, Jesus reached out to His accusers with reason. The essence of His argument was "I am not possessed by a demon" because "I honor my Father" (John 8:49). The point He made is impossible to miss: being demon-possessed and honoring God are *mutually exclusive*.

Finally, Scripture doesn't contain a single credible example of a demonized believer. Instead, the consistent teaching of the Bible is that Christians can't be controlled against their wills through demonic inhabitation. The principle is foolproof. If you're a follower of Christ, the King Himself indwells you. We can rest in the knowledge that "the one who is in you is greater than the one who is in the world" (1 John 4:4).

1 JOHN 4:4
"You, dear children, are from God and have overcome them, because the one who is in you is greater than the one who is in the world."

For further study, see Hank Hanegraaff, *The Covering: God's Plan to Protect You from Evil* (Nasville: W Publishing, 2002); and Hank Hanegraaff and Jay Strack, *The Covering: God's Plan to Protect You in the Midst of Spiritual Warfare*, Student Leadership University Study Guide Series (Nashville: Nelson Reference, 2006).

42

Can Satan Control Our Thoughts?

Satan can't interact directly with us in a physical sense. However, it is a mistake to assume that he doesn't have access to our minds.

First, Satan can't read our minds, but he *can* influence our thoughts. Because of this, the Bible instructs us to "put on the full armor of God so that you can take your stand against the devil's schemes" (Ephesians 6:11). Without it, you're a guaranteed casualty in this invisible war; but with it, you're invincible! Spiritual warfare is waged against invisible beings that personify the extremities of evil. Their weapons are spiritual, not physical. While they can't hurt us physically, violate us sexually, or cause us to levitate, they can tempt us to cheat, steal, and lie.

Furthermore, it's very important to know that if you open the door to sin by failing to put on God's full armor, Satan has the ability to sit on your shoulder and "whisper in your ear," so to speak. The whisper can't be discerned with the physical ear, but it can penetrate your mind.

We can't explain how this kind of communication takes place any more than we can explain how our immaterial minds cause the physical synapses of our brains to fire. But it's a fact that such communication takes place. If it weren't true, the devil couldn't have tempted Judas to betray his Master, encouraged Ananias and Sapphira to deceive Peter, or persuaded David to take a census.

Finally, while fallen angels aren't material beings and therefore can't interact with us directly in the physical sense, they're as real as the flesh on our bones. I don't doubt for a minute that the devil loves the way we so often depict him—as a cartoon-like clown with a long barbed tail, horns, red tights, and a pitchfork. Far from silly or stupid, however, Satan appears as a modern angel of enlightenment. He knows quite well that without our spiritual armor, we're pawns in his game. In a final look at Scripture, we're informed that spiritual warfare is the battle for the mind.

*"For our struggle is not against flesh and blood,
but against the rulers, against the authorities,
against the powers of this dark world and against the
spiritual forces of evil in the heavenly realms.
Therefore put on the full armor of God,
so that when the day of evil comes,
you may be able to stand your ground,
and after you have done everything, to stand."*

For further study, see Hank Hanegraaff and Jay Strack, *The Covering: God's Plan to Protect You in the Midst of Spiritual Warfare*, Student Leadership University Study Guide Series (Nashville: Nelson Reference, 2006); and C. S. Lewis, *The Screwtape Letters* (New York: Macmillan, 1982).

43

Are Generational Curses Biblical?

Based on texts taken out of context and used as pretexts, it has become increasingly common for Christians to believe they're victims of generational curses—that they've inherited demons ranging from anger to alcoholism, from laziness to lust. When we look at this idea closer, however, we see that it's seriously flawed.

First, Scripture clearly shows us that it is consequences, not curses, that are passed on through the generations. In this sense, the Bible says that children are punished for the sins of their fathers "to the third and fourth generation" (Exodus 20:5). The children of alcoholic fathers frequently suffer neglect and abuse as a direct consequence of their father's sinful behavior. Moreover, the descendants of those who hate God are likely to follow in the footsteps of their forefathers.

Scripture clearly tells us that "the son will not share the guilt of the father, nor will the father share the guilt of the son" (Ezekiel 18:20). When ancient Israel quoted the proverb, "The fathers eat sour grapes, and the children's teeth are set on edge" (v. 2). God responded in no uncertain terms: "As surely as I live, declares the Sovereign LORD, you will no longer quote this proverb in Israel.... The soul who sins is the one who will die" (vv. 3–4).

Finally, while the idea of generational curses is not contained in Scripture, there is a sense in which the curse of sin has been passed on from generation to generation: Through the first Adam, "all have sinned and fall short of the glory of God" (Romans 3:23). Through the Second Adam, Jesus Christ, atonement is offered to all. As Paul says, "Just as the result of one trespass was condemnation for all men, so also the result of one act of righteousness was justification that brings life for all men" (Romans 5:18). Through no act of our own we're condemned; likewise, through no act of our own we're saved (Romans 5:12–21).

"The soul who sins is the one who will die.
The son will not share the guilt of the father, nor will
the father share the guilt of the son.
The righteousness of the righteous man will be
credited to him, and the wickedness
of the wicked will be charged against him."

For further study, see Hank Hanegraaff, *The Covering: God's Plan to Protect You from Evil* (Nashville: W Publishing, 2002); and Hank Hanegraaff and Jay Strack, *The Covering: God's Plan to Protect You in the Midst of Spiritual Warfare*, Student Leadership University Study Guide Series (Nashville: Nelson Reference, 2006).

Scripture clearly tells us that "the son will not share the guilt of the father, nor will the father share the guilt of the son" (Ezekiel 18:20).

– 44 –

Does Human Cloning Fit into a Christian Worldview?

✳

A s has been well said, "The only thing necessary for evil to triumph is for good men to do nothing." The reality of this statement was carried out in 1973, when Christians quietly lost a major battle in the war against abortion. Two and a half decades later, the impact of that loss is still being felt, in ongoing debate over human cloning. While Pandora's box is already open, Christians must do everything permitted by Scripture to prevent a human clone from emerging.

First, the issues concerning cloning and abortion are closely interwoven. In other words, the logic that lets a woman terminate the life of her child in the womb may also apply equally to cloning. For example, if defects were detected in developing clones, abortion might be the automatic solution of choice.

Furthermore, producing a human clone would require experiments to be conducted on hundreds, if not thousands, of live human embryos. As a result, the entire process would be the moral equivalent of human experiments carried out by Nazi scientists under Adolf Hitler.

Finally, it should be noted that cloning has serious implications about what constitutes a family. While children are the result of spousal reproduction, clones are basically the result of scientific replication. This raises a troubling question: Who owns the clone? It's terrifying to think that the first human clone might be owned and operated by the very scientists who conduct such ghastly experiments.

JOB 33:4
*"The Spirit of God has made me;
the breath of the Almighty gives me life."*

For further study, see Hank Hanegraaff, *The F.A.C.E. That Demonstrates the Farce of Evolution* (Nashville: Word Publishing, 1998), "Human Cloning" and also "Annihilating Abortion Arguments"; see also The Center for Bioethics and Human Dignity, 2065 Half Day Road, Bannockburn, IL 60015, www.cbhd.org.

Should Christians Support a Ban on Embryonic Stem Cell Research?

✳

In 2004, the cash-strapped state of California passed Proposition 71, allocating $3 billion to finance the cloning of human embryos and their subsequent destruction through embryonic stem cell research. Support for this proposition was greatly influenced by celebrities like Brad Pitt, Nancy Reagan, and the late Christopher Reeve, who reiterated the biotech industry's promise that embryonic stem cell research would lead to cures for debilitating diseases and spinal cord injuries. Other celebrities like Mel Gibson and Joni Eareckson Tada (herself a quadriplegic) rightly responded that anyone who is concerned about the sanctity of human life must support a complete ban on the use of this technology.

First, make no mistake—extracting stem cells from an embryo kills the embryo. While an embryo doesn't have a fully developed personality, it does have full personhood from the moment of conception. You didn't *come from* an adolescent, you once *were* an adolescent; likewise, you didn't *come from* an embryo, you once *were* an embryo. All human beings are created in the image of God and endowed with the right to life, regardless of size, location, or level of dependency.

Furthermore, while we should sympathize with anyone who suffers from debilitating diseases or injuries, cures and therapies have to be sought within appropriate moral boundaries. Killing human embryos in the search for cures is just like subjecting one class of people to harmful experimentation for the sake of another. Doing this violates the biblical injunction against murdering humans made in the image of God (Genesis 1:26–27; 9:5–6), as well as the Nuremberg Code compiled by the tribunal responsible for judging the Nazis after World War II.

Finally, in light of the promising results of adult stem cell research, state funding for the destruction of embryos isn't just morally wrong; it's also financially irresponsible. Stem cells extracted from non-embryonic sources like bone marrow, blood, brain cells, and baby teeth are similar to embryonic stem cells in their ability to grow into multiple types of tissues. While embryonic stem cells used in research have demonstrated a tendency to grow into tumors, adult stem cells have already shown success in human trials for treatment of multiple sclerosis, sickle cell anemia, stroke, Parkinson's disease, and more.

The frightening conclusion is that the growing enthusiasm about embryonic stem cell research is more a pretext for human cloning than a context for responsible medical progress.

PROVERBS 24:11–12
"Rescue those being led away to death;
hold back those staggering toward slaughter.
If you say, 'But we knew nothing about this,' does not
he who weighs the heart perceive it? Does not he
who guards your life know it? Will he not repay each
person according to what he has done?"

For further study, see Charles W. Colson and Nigel M. de S. Cameron, *Human Dignity in the Biotech Century: A Christian Vision for Public Policy* (Downers Grove, Ill.: InterVarsity Press, 2004).

Anyone who is concerned
about the sanctity of
human life must support a
complete ban on the
use of this technology.

– 46 –

Should Abortion Be Allowed in Certain Situations, like Rape or Incest?

✳

W, hen the subject of abortion comes up, rape and incest are often used as an emotional appeal designed to deflect serious consideration of the pro-life position: "How could anyone force a hurting woman to carry a baby that resulted from the cruel and criminal invasion of her body?" The emotion of the argument often negates any serious examination of its merits.

First, it's important to know that the incidence of pregnancy as a result of rape is rare. Studies estimate that approximately 1 to 4.7 percent of rapes result in pregnancy. So lobbying for abortion on the basis of rape and incest is like lobbying for the removal of red lights because you might have to run one in order to rescue someone who's about to commit suicide. Even if we had legislation that restricted abortion for all reasons other than rape or incest, we would save the vast majority of the 1.8 million preborn babies who die annually in the United States through abortion.

Furthermore, we don't eliminate the real pain of rape or incest by compounding it with the murder of an innocent preborn child. Two wrongs don't make a right. The very thing that makes rape evil also makes abortion evil. In both cases, an innocent human being is brutally dehumanized.

But the real question is whether abortion is the murder of an innocent human being. If so, abortion should be avoided at all costs. In an age of scientific enlightenment, we now know that the embryo even at its earliest stages fulfills the criteria needed to establish the existence of biological life (including metabolism, development, ability to react to stimuli, and cell reproduction); that a zygote is a living human being as demonstrated by its distinct genetic code; and that human personhood doesn't depend on size, location, or level of dependence. Because of these facts, abortion should be avoided even in cases of rape and incest.

PROVERBS 17:15
"Acquitting the guilty and condemning the innocent—the LORD detests them both."

For further study, see Hank Hanegraaff, "Annihilating Abortion Arguments," available through the Christian Research Institute (CRI) at www.equip.org.

Is Capital Punishment Biblical?

✳

Both Christians who believe in capital punishment and Christians who don't use the Bible to support their beliefs. So what does the Bible really teach regarding capital punishment?

For starters, we need to recognize that in the very first book of the Bible God communicates His position clearly: "Whoever sheds the blood of man, by man shall his blood be shed; for in the image of God has God made man" (Genesis 9:6). It's instructive to note that this passage not only predates the Mosaic Law, but it demands total adherence to the sanctity of life.

Furthermore, in Exodus 21 and Deuteronomy 19 the Bible reaffirms God's perspective on capital punishment by emphasizing the principle of "life for life." To murder a person who is made in the image of God isn't just showing contempt for the apex of God's creation, but also contempt for the Creator Himself. Thus, while capital punishment may be in the wrong from a secular perspective, it is basic to a biblical worldview.

Finally, capital punishment is absolutely validated in the New Testament. Jesus acknowledged the legitimacy of capital punishment before Pilate (John 19:11), just as the apostle Paul did before the Roman governor Festus (Acts 25:11). Not only that, but one of the thieves crucified with Christ had the candor to confess, "We are punished justly, for we are getting what our deeds deserve" (Luke 23:41). And Romans 13 implies that the failure of the governing authorities to apply the "sword"—the Roman symbol for capital punishment—celebrates evil and erases justice.

In short, God instituted capital punishment in the earliest stages of human civilization before the Mosaic Law, and capital punishment is never annulled by Jesus or the apostles. Because of this, capital punishment appears to be an enduring moral principle supporting the sanctity of life.

GENESIS 9:5–6

*"And from each man, too, I will demand an
accounting for the life of his fellow man. Whoever
sheds the blood of man, by man shall his blood be
shed; for in the image of God has God made man."*

For further study, see Hank Hanegraaff, "Karla Faye Tucker and Capital
Punishment," available from CRI at www.equip.org; see also J. Daryl
Charles, "Sentiments as Social Justice: The Ethics of Capital Punishment,"
Christian Research Journal, spring/summer 1994.

While capital punishment
may be in the wrong
from a secular
perspective, it is
basic to a
biblical worldview.

– 48 –

Is the Bible Outdated in Its Views on Homosexuality?

✳

n light of the scientific age we live in, it's a popular sentiment to view the Bible as "outdated." And when Scripture's condemnation of homosexuality is used in an argument, it's not uncommon to see expressions of annoyance or exasperation on people's faces. After all, the Bible condemns not only homosexuality but also anyone who breaks the Sabbath (Exodus 35:2).

First, it should be noted that while Sabbath-breaking carried serious punishment in ancient Israel, it isn't a reason to execute people today. Not only are we no longer under the civil and ceremonial laws of Jewish theocratic government, but as the apostle Paul explains, the symbolism of the Law has been fulfilled in Christ (Galatians 3:13–14). In his letter to the Colossians, Paul reminds us that we're free of having to follow Sabbath laws: "These are a shadow of the things that were to come; the reality, however, is found in Christ" (Colossians 2:17). Thus, there is an obvious difference between enduring moral principles regarding homosexuality and temporary civil and ceremonial laws relegated to a particular historical context.

Furthermore, we should recognize that the God of the Bible doesn't condemn homosexuality in a random or fickle way. Rather, He carefully defines the boundaries of human sexuality *so that our joy may be complete*. It doesn't take a rocket scientist to see that our bodies aren't designed for homosexual relationships. Popular slogans and emotional arguments don't change the scientific reality that homosexual relationships are damaging not just psychologically but also physiologically.

The Old Testament's warning against homosexuality is far from outdated; in fact, it is eerily prophetic. As we read in the book of Romans, "Their women exchanged natural relations for unnatural ones. In the same way the men also abandoned natural relations with women and were inflamed with lust for one another. Men committed indecent acts with other men, and *received in themselves the due penalty for their perversion*" (Romans 1:26–27, emphasis added).

It's pretty hard to miss the relationship between Paul's words and the current health-care crisis. More people have already died of AIDS than the U.S. has lost in all wars combined. And that's just the tip of the iceberg. The homosexual lifestyle triggers a number of complications, including hemorrhoids, prostate damage, and infectious fissures. Nonviral infections transmitted through homosexual activity include gonorrhea, chlamydia, and syphilis, while viral infections include condylomata, herpes, and hepatitis A and B.

While there are moral and medical problems associated with sexual promiscuity in general, it would be extremely homophobic to obscure the scientific realities concerning homosexuality. It's a horrendous hate crime to attempt to keep a whole segment of the population in the dark concerning these issues. Thus, far from showing the Bible to be out of step with the times, its warnings regarding homosexuality demonstrate that it is as relevant today as it was in the beginning.

ROMANS 1:26–27

"Even their women exchanged natural relations
for unnatural ones. In the same way
the men also abandoned natural relations with
women and were inflamed with lust for one another.
Men committed indecent acts with other men,
and received in themselves the due penalty
for their perversion."

For further study, see Joe Dallas, *A Strong Delusion: Confronting the "Gay Christian" Movement* (Eugene, Ore.: Harvest House Publishers, 1996). See also Hank Hanegraaff, "President Bartlett's Fallacious Diatribe," available at www.equip.org.

What's the Problem with Pornography?

✴

Today, sexually explicit images are as accessible as the click of a mouse. Consequently, pornography has become pandemic. As Joe Dallas observed, pornography is not only an enslaving addiction and a violation of marriage vows, but a precursor to increasingly dangerous and degrading sexual practices.

First, pornography is an addictive behavior that enslaves the mind and conditions users to see others as objects of self-gratification. Jesus warned us to guard our gaze: "The eye is the lamp of the body. If your eyes are good, your whole body will be full of light. But if your eyes are bad, your whole body will be full of darkness. If then the light within you is darkness, how great is that darkness!" (Matthew 6:22–23).

Furthermore, pornography breaks the sacred bond of marriage and tears apart the very fabric of society. When pornographic images are used to satisfy sexual desire, a marriage partner is defrauded. Even if you are not yet married your future husband or wife is harmed and violated if you use pornography. In the

152 THE BIBLE ANSWER BOOK FOR STUDENTS

Sermon on the Mount, Jesus said that lustful visual encounters were the moral equivalent of extramarital sex (Matthew 5:28).

Finally, just like smoking marijuana often leads to more dangerous drugs, so pornography often leads to increasingly deviant sexual behaviors. Says James: "Each one is tempted when, by his own evil desire, he is dragged away and enticed. Then, after desire has conceived, it gives birth to sin; and sin, when it is full-grown, gives birth to death" (James 1:14–15).

Thankfully, even the strongest addiction to pornography can be overcome by taking these practical steps to remove the temptation: establish an accountability structure, and put on the full armor of God (Ephesians 6:10–20). The "covering" described in Scripture as the full armor of God is an impenetrable barrier, and the fiery darts of the evil one are impotent against it. When we're clothed in the covering, we're invincible. But when we're not, we become pawns in the devil's malevolent schemes.

"No temptation has seized you except what is common to man. And God is faithful; he will not let you be tempted beyond what you can bear. But when you are tempted, he will also provide a way out so that you can stand up under it."

For further study, see Joe Dallas, "Darkening Our Minds: The Problem of Pornography Among Christians," *Christian Research Journal* 27, 3 (2004): 12–21.

When we're clothed in
the full armor of God,
we're invincible.

Should Christians Use Birth Control?

n light of recent advances in biotechnology, it's important to look at the issue of birth control through the filter of the Bible.

There is much debate among Christians about whether birth control is appropriate in any form. But first, there is no question that birth control methods designed to destroy or prevent the implantation of a fertilized egg (i.e., embryo) should be avoided at all costs. From the moment of conception, an embryo is a living, growing person made in the image of God (Genesis 1:26–27; 9:6; Exodus 20:13). Thus, the "abortion pill" (RU486) must *never* be used. Similarly, the "morning-after pill" and oral contraceptives (i.e., the birth-control pill) must not be used because they are designed to prevent not only fertilization but also uterine implantation if fertilization should occur.

Furthermore, the necessary openness to children that accompanies sexual union protects us as Christians from abusing sex for mere self-gratification. When birth-control methods are employed out of a selfish unwillingness to have children, sex can quickly degenerate into nothing more than what Oxford professor Olive O'Donovan has aptly described as "a profound form of play."

Finally, the use of birth control never justifies engaging in premarital sex. Abstaining from sex until you're married is the only way to fully experience and enjoy God's perfect design for sexual intimacy. Abstinence is also the only way to effectively prevent teenage pregnancy and the numerous psychological, emotional, and physical consequences of premarital sex (including STDs). To treat sex in a casual way by engaging in sexual intercourse without a marital commitment harms those who do so, violates the trust of future spouses, and pains our heavenly Father.

*"Then little children were brought to Jesus
for him to place his hands on them and pray for
them. But the disciples rebuked those who
brought them. Jesus said, 'Let the little children come
to me, and do not hinder them, for the
kingdom of heaven belongs to such as these.'"*

For further study, see Randy Alcorn, *Does the Birth Control Pill Cause
Abortion?* 7th ed. (Gresham, Ore.: Eternal Perspective Ministries, 1997).

From the moment
of conception,
an embryo is a living,
growing person made in
the image of God.

51

Is Suicide an Unforgivable Sin?

✳

I n our society of stressed-out people, suicide isn't merely a secular problem, nor is it a problem for one particular group of people. According to the Centers for Disease Control, suicide is the third-leading cause of death among young people ages fifteen to twenty-four. As the number of suicides continues to skyrocket, I am frequently asked whether suicide is an unforgivable sin.

First, no single act is unforgivable. The only unforgivable sin is a *continuous, ongoing* rejection of forgiveness. Those who refuse forgiveness through Christ will spend eternity separated from His love and grace. Conversely, those who sincerely desire forgiveness can be absolutely certain that God will never spurn them.

Furthermore, while suicide is not an unforgivable sin, those who take the sacred name of Christ upon their lips dare not contemplate it. Our lives belong to God, and only He has the prerogative to bring them to an end. In the words of the Almighty, "See now that I myself am He! There is no god besides me.

I put to death and I bring to life, I have wounded and I will heal, and no one can deliver out of my hand" (Deuteronomy 32:39, emphasis added).

Finally, suicide is the murder of oneself and is therefore a direct violation of the sixth commandment—"You shall not murder" (Exodus 20:13; cf. Genesis 9:6). Without a doubt, suicide is a direct attack on the sovereignty of the very One who knit us together in our mothers' wombs (Psalm 139:13).

REVELATION 21:8
"But the cowardly, the unbelieving, the vile, the murderers, the sexually immoral, those who practice magic arts, the idolaters and all liars—their place will be in the fiery lake of burning sulfur. This is the second death."

52

Is It Ever Okay to Lie?

In the interest of truth, I want to first say that Christian theologians are divided on this subject. Some, like Saint Augustine, believe that it is never okay to lie. Others, like Dietrich Bonhoeffer, who had ample time to contemplate this issue from the perspective of a Nazi prison cell, hold that under certain circumstances lying wasn't just okay, but a moral responsibility. Bonhoeffer believed in deceiving the enemy in circumstances of war, and he had no guilt about lying in order to help Jews escape extermination.

Furthermore, while the Bible never condones lying for the sake of lying, it does condone lying in order to preserve a higher moral imperative. For example, Rahab purposed to deceive (the lesser moral law) in order to save the lives of two Jewish spies (the higher moral law). In the same way, a Christian father today shouldn't hesitate to lie in order to protect his wife and daughters from being raped or murdered.

It's important to understand that there's a difference between *lying* and *not telling the truth*.

It isn't just a matter of wording; it's a matter of substance. As an example, there is a difference between unjustified and justified homicide. Murder is unjustified homicide and is always wrong; however, not every instance of killing a person is murder. Capital punishment and self-defense sometimes justify homicide.

Similarly, in the case of a lie (Ananias and Sapphira in Acts 5), there is an unjustified discrepancy between what you believe and what you say, and so *lying* is always wrong. But *not telling the truth* in order to preserve a higher moral law (Rahab in Joshua 2) may actually be the right thing to do, and because of this it isn't a lie.

*"The king of Jericho sent this message to Rahab:
'Bring out the men who came to you
and entered your house, because they have come
to spy out the whole land.' But the woman had taken
the two men and hidden them. She said,
'Yes, the men came to me, but I did not know
where they had come from. At dusk, when it was
time to close the city gate, the men left. I don't
know which way they went. Go after them quickly.
You may catch up with them.' (But she had taken
them up to the roof and hidden them under
the stalks of flax she had laid out on the roof.)"*

For further study, see Norman L. Geiser, *Christian Ethics: Options and Issues* (Grand Rapids: Baker Book House, 1989), chapter 7.

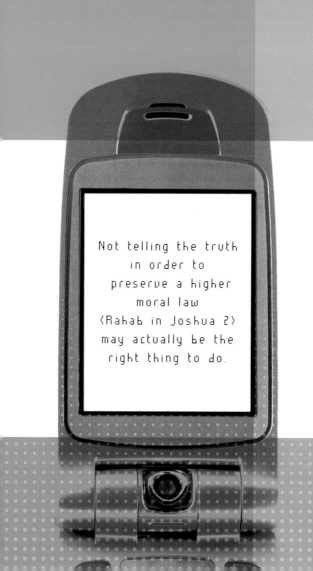

Not telling the truth in order to preserve a higher moral law (Rahab in Joshua 2) may actually be the right thing to do.

−53−

What Is a Cult?

✳

L arry King asked me this question after thirty-nine people took their lives in the largest mass suicide in U.S. history; he went on to ask me whether Christianity might legitimately be referred to as a cult. As I explained on *Larry King Live*, the word *cult* has various connotations.

First, a cult may be defined *sociologically*. From this perspective, a cult is a religious or semi-religious sect whose followers are controlled by strong leadership in virtually every dimension of their lives. Followers generally display a displaced loyalty for the guru and the group and are galvanized together through physical and/or psychological intimidation tactics. This kind of cultist more often than not has a "we/they" siege mentality and has been cut off from all former relationships, including their immediate families.

A cult may also be defined *theologically*. In this sense, a cult can be a pseudo-Christian organization that claims to be Christian but compromises, confuses, or contradicts essential Christian doctrine.

These kinds of cults operate under the guise of Christianity, but they deviate from the orthodox teachings of the historic Christian faith as given in ancient ecumenical creeds. Typically, followers become masters at taking texts out of context to develop pretexts for theological distortions.

Finally, I should note that although the media-driven culture has given the term *cult* a highly negative connotation, denotatively the word *cult* can be broadly defined as a group of people centered around a religious belief structure. In this light, Christianity could rightly be referred to as a "cult of Old Testament Judaism." In fact, the Latin verb *cultus* from which we derive the word *cult* simply means "to worship a deity." So in dealing with cults, it's important to thoroughly define terms.

"But I am afraid that just as Eve was deceived by the serpent's cunning, your minds may somehow be led astray from your sincere and pure devotion to Christ. For if someone comes to you and preaches a Jesus other than the Jesus we preached, or if you receive a different spirit from the one you received, or a different gospel from the one you accepted, you put up with it easily enough."

For further study, see Hank Hanegraaff, *Counterfeit Revival*, rev. ed. (Nashville: Word Publishing Group, 2001), part 5; and Ron Rhodes, *The Challenge of the Cults and New Religions* (Grand Rapids: Zondervan, 2001).

In dealing
with cults,
it's important
to thoroughly
define terms.

54

Are Jehovah's Witnesses Christian?

✳

Like Mormons, Jehovah's Witnesses believe that Christianity died with the last of the apostles. They also believe Christianity wasn't resurrected until their founder, Charles Taze Russell, began organizing the Watchtower Society in the 1870s. In their view, the cross is a pagan symbol adopted by an apostate church, and salvation is impossible apart from the Watchtower. While the Witnesses on your doorstep consider themselves to be the only authentic expression of Christianity, the Society they serve compromises, confuses, and contradicts essential Christian doctrine.

First, the Watchtower Society compromises the nature of God. They teach their devotees that the Trinity is a "freakish-looking, three headed God" invented by Satan and that Jesus is merely a god. In Watchtower theology, Jesus was created by God as the archangel Michael, during His time on earth became merely human, and after His crucifixion was re-created as an "immaterial spirit creature." JWs also deny the physical resurrection of Jesus. According to Russell, the body that hung on a torture stake either "dissolved into gases" or is "preserved somewhere as the grand memorial of God's love."

Furthermore, while Christians believe all believers will spend eternity with Christ in "a new heaven and a new earth" (Revelation 21:1), the Watchtower teaches that only 144,000 people will make it to heaven while the rest of the faithful will live apart from Christ on earth. So in Watchtower lore, there's a "little flock" of 144,000 who get to go to heaven, and a "great crowd" of others who are relegated to earth. The heavenly class are born again, receive the baptism of the Holy Spirit, and take communion; the earthly class don't. To substantiate the notion that heaven's door was closed forever in 1935, JWs point to "flashes of prophetic light" received by Joseph F. Rutherford at a JW convention in Washington DC. Other false "flashes of prophetic light" include Watchtower predictions of end-time cataclysms that were to occur in 1914…1918…1925…1975.

Finally, under the threat of being "disfellowshipped," Jehovah's Witnesses don't celebrate Christmas, birthdays, or holidays such as Thanksgiving or Good Friday. Even more troubling are the

Watchtower regulations regarding vaccinations, organ transplants, and blood transfusions. In 1931, JWs were instructed to refuse vaccinations—but by 1952, this regulation was withdrawn. In 1967, organ transplants were ruled a forbidden form of cannibalism—but by 1980, this edict was erased. In 1909, the Watchtower produced a prohibition against blood transfusions. No doubt, this, too, will one day become a relic of the past. In the meantime, tens of thousands not only have been robbed spiritually by the Watchtower Society but have paid the ultimate physical price as well.

Even though Watchtower adherents are often willing to do more for a lie than Christians are willing to do for the truth, these and many other doctrinal perversions keep JWs from rightly being considered Christian.

DEUTERONOMY 18:22

"If what a prophet proclaims in the name of the LORD does not take place or come true, that is a message the LORD has not spoken. That prophet has spoken presumptuously. Do not be afraid of him."

For further study, see Ron Rhodes, *Reasoning from the Scriptures with the Jehovah's Witnesses* (Eugene, Ore.: Harvest House Publishers, 1993).

The Watchtower Society
compromises the nature of God.

55

Is Mormonism Christian?

T he Church of Jesus Christ of Latter-day Saints was birthed in 1820 by an alleged vision in which two celestial personages appeared to Joseph Smith, claiming *all* existing churches were wrong, *all* their creeds were an abomination, and *all* their professors were corrupt. According to these personages, Smith had been chosen to *restore*—not *reform*—a church that had disappeared from the face of the earth. The Mormon doctrines that evolved from this vision compromise, confuse, and contradict the nature of God, the authority of Scripture, and the way of salvation.

First, while Christians believe that God is spirit (John 4:24), Joseph Smith taught, "God Himself was once as we are now, and is an exalted man, and sits enthroned in yonder heavens!" Mormonism also holds to a plurality of gods and contends that "as man is, God once was; as God is, man may become." Additionally, the Latter-day Saints compromise the nature of the God-man, Jesus Christ. In Christianity, Jesus is the self-existent Creator of all things

(Colossians 1:15–20). In Mormonism, He is the spirit brother of Lucifer who was conceived in heaven by a celestial Mother and came in flesh as the result of the Father having sex with the Virgin Mary.

Furthermore, in sharp distinction to orthodox Christian theology, Mormons don't believe that the Bible is *infallible* (2 Timothy 3:16). In their view, the *Book of Mormon* is "the most correct of any book on earth, and the keystone of our religion." Two further revelations complete the Mormon quad, *Doctrine and Covenants* and *The Pearl of Great Price. Doctrine and Covenants* is a collection of divine revelations that includes the doctrine of polygamy. It wasn't until Mormons were threatened by the federal government that the Mormon president, Wilford Woodruff, received a "revelation" downgrading polygamy to the afterlife. *The Pearl of Great Price* is just as troubling; this extra-biblical revelation was used by Mormonism to prevent African-Americans from entering the priesthood and from being exalted to godhood.

Finally, while Christians believe that they'll stand before God dressed in the "spotless robes of Christ's righteousness" (see Romans 3:21–22; Philippians 3:9), Mormons claim they'll appear before the heavenly Father dressed in fig-leaf aprons holding good works in their hands. According to the Latter-day Saints, virtually everyone qualifies for heaven. Murderers, unrepentant whoremongers, and the world's vilest people make it into the *Telestial heaven*; lukewarm Mormons, religious people, and those who accept the Mormon gospel in the spirit world typically enter the *Terrestrial heaven*; and temple Mormons make it to the *Celestial heaven*. Only those who are sealed in secret temple rituals, however, will make it to the third level of the Celestial kingdom and become gods of their own planets.

These and many other doctrinal perversions exclude Mormonism from rightly being called Christian.

ISAIAH 43:10

"'You are my witnesses,' declares the LORD,
'and my servant whom I have chosen,
so that you may know and believe me and understand
that I am he. Before me no god was formed,
nor will there be one after me.'"

For further study, see Richard Abanes, *One Nation Under Gods* (New York: Four Walls Eight Windows, 2003).

Mormonism holds to a plurality of gods and contends that "as man is, God once was; as God is, man may become."

Is Seventh Day Adventisim Orthodox?

ver the years, I've met many Seventh Day Adventists who told me that worshiping on Sunday is taking the mark of the Beast. Far from being monolithic, however, Seventh Day Adventism is multifaceted.

First, there are Adventists who are thoroughly orthodox. As such, they embrace the essentials of the historic Christian faith. While we may vigorously debate secondary issues, we're unified around the essentials for which martyrs shed blood.

Furthermore, there are Adventists who are thoroughly liberal. They not only compromise and confuse facts, but they also contradict essentials of the faith like the virgin birth, the bodily resurrection, and the infallibility of Scripture.

Finally, there are traditionalists who believe in deviant doctrines like soul sleep, Sabbatarianism, and the seer status of Ellen G. White. In sharp distinction to soul sleep, the Bible provides ample evidence that the soul continues to exist apart from the body (Philippians 1:23–24). God Himself provided early

Christians with a new pattern of worship through Christ's resurrection on the first day of the week as well as the Spirit's descent on Pentecost Sunday. Additionally, while Ellen White (1827–1915) claimed divine authority for her prophecies, she was obviously wrong when she prophesied that she would be alive at the second coming of Christ.

HEBREWS 4:9–10

"There remains then, a Sabbath-rest
for the people of God; for anyone who enters
God's rest also rests from his own work,
just as God did from his."

For further study, see Hank Hanegraaff, "Why do Christians worship on Sunday rather than on the Sabbath day?" and "Is there evidence for life after death?" *The Bible Answer Book Volume 1* (Nashville: J. Countryman, 2004), 70–72, 165–69.

What Do Hindus Believe?

✳

W hile Hinduism is multifaceted rather than monolithic, its basic tenets with respect to God, humanity, and salvation can be summed up in the next few paragraphs.

First, Hindus believe that ultimate reality (*Brahman*) is an impersonal oneness that transcends all distinctions, including personal and propositional differentiations. To put it another way, all of reality is a continuum, or a simplified whole, so there's no distinction between morals and mice.

Hindus also believe that humans, along with the rest of the universe, are a continuous extension of *Brahman*. Therefore, our "illusory individuated selves" (*atman*) are one with the impersonal cosmic consciousness of the universe—"*atman* is *Brahman* and *Brahman* is *atman*."

Finally, the Hindu scriptures (*Vedas* and *Upanishads*) teach the goal of humanity is liberation from an endless cycle of death and reincarnation (*samsara*). Liberation (*moksha*) from *samsara* is attained when we "realize" that our individual selves are an illusion, and all is one. Until such enlightenment is achieved, the law of *karma* dictates that a person's deeds in previous lives determine whether he is reborn as man, monkey, or mosquito; or as a woman, walrus, or wasp.

Where the Hindu scriptures tout the hell of reincarnation, the Holy Scriptures teach the hope of resurrection. The solution to the fear of karmic reincarnation is simple: faith in our Kinsman-Redeemer.

ISAIAH 44:24–25

"This is what the LORD says—your Redeemer,
who formed you in the womb;
I am the LORD, who has made all things,
who alone stretched out the heavens, who spread
out the earth by myself, who foils the
signs of false prophets and makes fools of diviners,
who overthrows the learning of the wise
and turns it into nonsense."

For further study, see Dean Halverson, *The Illustrated Guide to World Religions* (Minneapolis: Bethany House Publishers, 2003).

What Are the Basic Beliefs of Buddhism?

✳

T he year was 1893. The place was Chicago. Buddhists had arrived from the East to attend the inaugural World's Parliament of Religions. While their group was sizable, they were vastly outnumbered by Bible believers from the West. One hundred years later, at the centennial celebration of the original Parliament, Buddhists greatly outnumbered Baptists, and saffron robes were more common than Christian clerical clothing.

Given its growing impact, it's important to understand the basic beliefs of Buddhists and use them as springboards for sharing the liberating truth of the gospel.

First of all, Buddhism—a historical offshoot of Hinduism—teaches its followers to seek refuge in the Three Jewels: *Buddha*, *Dharma*, and *Sangha*. Embracing the triple gem means finding refuge in Buddha, who became the "enlightened one" for this age during a deep state of meditation under a bodhi tree; finding refuge in the Buddha's teaching—*dharma*; and finding refuge in the community of

Buddhist priests—*sangha*—who guide devotees along the path to enlightenment.

The essence of Buddhism is summed up in what they call the Four Noble Truths: 1) all life is suffering (*dukkha*); 2) the source of suffering is desire and attachment because all is impermanent; 3) liberation from suffering is found in the elimination of desire; 4) desire is eliminated by following the eightfold path.

Finally, the Eightfold Path is made up of right understanding, right thought, right speech, right action, right livelihood, right effort, right awareness, and right meditation. By following this path through many reincarnations, Buddhists hope to erase karmic debt and achieve *nirvana* ("no self"), gaining freedom from suffering and escaping the endless cycle of life, death, and rebirth (*samsara*).

In sharp contrast to the Buddhist teaching that we must *eliminate* desire, the Bible teaches that we must be disciplined in order to *transform* our desires (Romans 6:17–19). Ultimately, suffering isn't overcome through stamping out the self; it can only be found through the selfless sacrifice of a sinless Savior.

ROMANS 5:1–15

"Therefore, since we have been justified through faith, we have peace with God through our Lord Jesus Christ, through whom we have gained access by faith into this grace in which we now stand. And we rejoice in the hope of the glory of God. Not only so, but we also rejoice in our sufferings, because we know that suffering produces perseverance; perseverance, character; and character, hope. And hope does not disappoint us, because God has poured out his love into our hearts by the Holy Spirit, whom he has given us."

For further study, see J. Isamu Yamamoto's four-part *Christian Research Journal* series on Buddhism in North America, available through the Christian Research Institute (CRI) at www.equip.org.

In sharp contrast to the Buddhist
teaching that we must
eliminate desire, the Bible teaches
that we must be disciplined in order
to transform our desires.

59

What Is Judaism?

✳

While Judaism got its start through Abraham, Isaac, and Jacob, its modern-day expression is largely a function of the destruction of the temple in AD 70. As such, Judaism now finds expression in Torah study rather than temple sacrifice. The three main branches of Judaism are Orthodox, Reform, and Conservative.

Orthodox Judaism (Torah Judaism) is probably known best for its strict dedication to the eternal and unalterable Mosaic Law as reinterpreted by rabbis following the fall of Jerusalem. In this tradition, it's only through devotion to the complex code of Jewish law (*Halakhah*) that one can experience nearness to God. Orthodox Jews are waiting for a rebuilt temple, a Jewish Messiah who will restore the kingdom to Israel, and the physical resurrection of the dead. Ironically, it's possible to be an Orthodox Jew and yet not believe in the God of Abraham, Isaac, and Jacob.

Unlike Orthodox Judaism, which teaches that observance of the Law leads to freedom, Reform

Judaism (Liberal) begins with the freedom to decide what Law to observe. In other words, human autonomy trumps the authority of *Halakhah*. A movement that rose to prominence in the eighteenth century, Reform Judaism seeks to adapt to the modern world in order to preserve Jewish identify in the middle of pressure to conform. Thus, Reform Judaism is always changing.

Conservative Judaism (Historical) is a late–nineteenth-century reaction to the liberal tendencies inherent in Reform Judaism. This type of Judaism is a sort of "middle ground" between Orthodox and Reform Judaism. On the one hand, its followers embrace modern culture like Reformists; on the other, they follow Jewish laws and customs without the fundamentalistic fervor of the Orthodox.

No matter what religious affiliation is claimed by people we witness to, our duty is to demonstrate the reality of Jesus Christ through the testimony of our love, our life, and our lips. As the apostle Paul explains, the gospel of Jesus Christ "is the power of God for the salvation of everyone who believes: first for the Jews, then for the Gentile. For in the gospel a righteousness from God is revealed, a righteousness that is by faith from first to last, just as it is written: 'The righteous will live by faith'" (Romans 1:16–17).

*"He said to them, 'This is what I told you
while I was still with you:
Everything must be fulfilled that is
written about me in the Law of Moses,
the Prophets and the Psalms.'"*

For further study, see Richard Robinson, "Understanding Judaism: How to Share the Gospel with Your Jewish Friends," *Christian Research Journal* 19, 4 (1997), available through the Christian Research Institute (CRI) at www.equip.org.

No matter what religious affiliation is claimed by people we witness to, our duty is to demonstrate the reality of Jesus Christ through the testimony of our love, our life, and our lips.

60

Is the Allah of Islam the God of the Bible?

✳

Long before Muhammad was born, Arabic Christians already were referring to God as *Allah*—and millions continue to do so today. The Allah of Islam, however, is definitely not the God of the Bible. For while Muslims passionately defend the unity of God, they deny His triunity. They flinch at the notion of God as Father, reject the unique deity of Jesus Christ the Son, and renounce the divine identity of the Holy Spirit.

First, while the Master taught His disciples to pray "Our Father in heaven," followers of Muhammad find the very idea offensive. To their way of thinking, calling God "Father" and Jesus Christ "Son" suggests spiritual procreation. According to the Qur'an, "It is not befitting to (the majesty of) Allah that He should beget a son" (Sura 19:35), Allah "begetteth not, nor is he begotten" (Sura 112:3).

The Bible, however, doesn't use the term "begotten" with respect to the Father and the Son in the sense of sexual reproduction, but rather in the sense of special relationship. So when the apostle John speaks of Jesus as "the only *begotten* of the Father" (John 1:14 NKJV, emphasis added), he is talking about the unique deity of Christ. In the same way, when the apostle Paul refers to Jesus as "the *firstborn* over all creation" (Colossians 1:15, emphasis added), he is referring to Christ's preeminence or prime position as the Creator of *all* things (vv. 1:16–19). Christians are sons of God through adoption; Jesus is God the Son from all eternity.

Furthermore, Muslims dogmatically denounce the Christian declaration of Christ's unique deity as the unforgivable sin of shirk. As the Qur'an puts it, "god forgiveth not the sin of joining other gods with Him; but He forgiveth whom He pleaseth other sins than this" (Sura 4:116). While Muslims readily affirm the sinlessness of Christ, they adamantly deny His sacrifice upon the cross and subsequent resurrection. In doing so, they deny the single historic fact which demonstrates that Jesus doesn't stand in a long line of peers from Abraham to Muhammad, but is God in human flesh. The Qur'anic phrase "Allah raised him up" (Surah 4:158) is taken to mean that Jesus was supernaturally raptured rather than resurrected from the dead. In Islamic lore, God made someone look like Jesus, and this look-alike was crucified in His place. In recent years, the myth that Judas was crucified in place of Jesus has been popularized in Muslim circles by a late medieval invention titled the Gospel of Barnabas. Against the weight of history and evidence the Qur'an exudes, "they killed him not, nor crucified him, but so it was made to appear to them" (Sura 4:157).

Finally, in addition to rejecting Jesus' divinity, Islam also rejects the divine identity of the Holy Spirit. Far from being the third person of the Triune God who inspired the text of the Bible, the Holy Spirit—according to Islam—is the archangel Gabriel who dictated the Qur'an to Muhammad over a period of twenty-three years. Ironically, while the Holy Spirit who dictated the Qur'an is said to be the archangel Gabriel, Islam identifies the Holy Spirit promised by Jesus in John 14 as Muhammad. The Bible, however, rejects these corruptions and misrepresentation. Biblically, the Holy Spirit is neither an angel nor a mere mortal; rather, He is the very God who redeems us from our sins and will one day resurrect us to life eternal (Romans 8:11).

1 JOHN 2:23

"No one who denies the Son has the Father;
whoever acknowledges the Son has the Father also."

For further study, see Timothy George, *Is the Father of Jesus the God of Muhammad?* (Grand Rapids: Zondervan, 2002).

61

What Is Scientology?

Τ he Church of Scientology was founded in the 1950s by science-fiction author Lafayette Ronald (L. Ron) Hubbard. Although the church claims to be compatible with Christianity, the two belief structures—one rooted in science fiction, the other in soteriological fact— are contradictory and can't be harmonized.

First, Scientology teaches that humans are immortal *thetans* trapped in a physical universe of their own mental construction. In other words, humans aren't sinners in need of a savior, but immortal beings who can overcome enslaving *engrams*—the accumulation of trillions of years of painful subconscious memories—through the pseudo-psychology of *auditing*—the counseling process through which devotees can locate and resolve past traumatic experiences and gain spiritual enlightenment. As such, Scientology is a rejection of the biblical doctrines of creation, original sin, and exclusive salvation through Jesus Christ (cf. Genesis 1–3; John 14:6; Romans 3:23; 6:23).

Furthermore, Scientology holds that, apart from auditing, a continuous cycle of *reincarnation* (or "rebirth") is ahead for each of us. In order to escape this vicious cycle, we have to become "self-actualized" through the pseudo-psychology of Scientology. No religion that teaches self-actualization by escape from the body can be reconciled with the Christian belief in bodily perfection, purification, and preservation through resurrection (1 Corinthians 15).

Finally, despite allowing its adherents to believe in a god of their own choosing, Scientology champions a *Supreme Being* that bears a remarkable resemblance to the Brahman of Hinduism.

While L. Ron Hubbard's Supreme Being is science fiction and ultimately can't heal our pain, the Supreme Being of the Bible is able to stem Scientology's "trail of tears"—*Thetans, Engrams, Auditing, Reincarnation, Supreme Being*—and meet our deepest needs.

*"Even from your own number men will arise
and distort the truth in order to draw away disciples
after them. So be on your guard! Remember
that for three years I never stopped
warning each of you night and day with tears."*

For further study, see John Weldon, "Scientology: From Science Fiction to Space-Age Religion," *Christian Research Journal* 16, 1 (1993), available through the Christian Research Institute (CRI) at www.equip.org.

Scientology's philosophy leaves a trail of tears:

Thetans—immortal state of humans

Engrams—accumulation of painful subconscious memories

Auditing—counseling process for identifying and overcoming engrams and achieving enlightenment

Reincarnation—cycle of rebirth to be repeated until self-actualization

Supreme Being—a god remarkably like the Brahman of Hinduism

No religion that teaches self-actualization by escape from the body can be reconciled with the Christian belief in bodily perfection, purification, and preservation through resurrection (1 Corinthians 15).

– 6 2 –

What's Wrong with Wicca?

✳

Wicca is a neo-pagan, earth-centered religion that has its modern origins in the teaching and practice of the original English Wiccan, Gerald Gardner (1884–1964). Today, Wicca is experiencing dramatic growth as teens reject what they perceive as Christian paternalism, homophobia, and insensitivity to the environment. While stereotypes of Wiccans as Satanists or sinister spell-casters are false, the worldviews of Christianity and Wicca are still worlds apart.

First, Wicca, also known as "The Craft" or "The Old Religion," teaches that all reality is divine. Thus, Wiccans revere the natural world as a living, breathing organism, and they revere people as "gods" and "goddesses." Because Wicca is a distinctively feminist form of neo-paganism, however, Wiccans often consider the supreme manifestation of deity to be a nature goddess (such as the Triple Goddess of the Moon).

In sharp contrast to the Christian worldview, Wiccans worship creation rather than the Creator (cf. Romans 1:25). While the Bible does teach that people should care for the environment (Genesis 2:15; Deuteronomy 20:19–20; Psalm 115:16) and appreciate its magnificence (Psalm 19; Matthew 6:28–30), our worship belongs only to the Creator, whose glory is reflected in His creation (Job 38–41; Psalm 148; Romans 1).

Furthermore, the supreme ethical rule of Wicca is the Wiccan Rede: "If it harms none, do as ye Will." Despite this advice not to harm others, Wiccans believe that moral and religious truths are ultimately relative. So while the Wiccan Rede sets the Craft apart from the wicked activities of Satanists, the Wiccan worldview is in direct opposition to the biblical notions of absolute moral truth and exclusive salvation through Jesus Christ, who alone is "the way and the truth and the life" (John 14:6).

Finally, Wiccans practice magick (spelled with a *k* to differentiate it from conjuring for entertainment) in an attempt to manipulate the natural world and alter mental and material conditions. Because of this, Wicca is an occult practice designed to make reality look like the Wiccans' will. Tools of the Craft include swords and spell books, chalices, censers, cords, and crystals.

Regardless of whether the motivation is good or evil, Scripture unquestionably condemns all occult practices as being detestable to the Lord (Deuteronomy 18:10–12; Acts 13:6–11; 16:16–18; Galatians 5:19–21).

DEUTERONOMY 18:10–11

"Let no one be found among you
who sacrifices his son or daughter in the fire,
who practices divination or sorcery, interprets omens,
engages in witchcraft, or casts spells, or who
is a medium or spiritist or who consults the dead."

For further study, see Richard G. Howe, "Modern Witchcraft: It may not be what you think," *Christian Research Journal* 28, 1 (2005); 12–21, available through the Christian Research Institute (CRI) at www.equip.org.

The Wiccan worldview is in direct opposition to the biblical notions of absolute moral truth and exclusive salvation through Jesus Christ, who alone is "the way and the truth and the life" (John 14:6).

What Is the Occult?

While the word *occult* (from the Latin "ocultus") means "hidden" or "secret," the world of the occult is clearly out in the open. It's been glamorized as New Age, but its origin is as age-old as the hiss of the serpent: "Your eyes will be opened, and you will be like God, knowing good and evil" (Genesis 3:5). The objective of occultism is self-deification through sorcery, spiritism, and soothsaying.

First, through sorcery (magick), occultists seek to harness paranormal powers for their own purposes. Using ritualistic formulas, spells, and incantations, occultists seek to harness what they perceive to be the natural and spiritual powers of the universe to satisfy their personal desires. God warned the ancient Israelites that these very practices would lead to their downfall (Deuteronomy 18:9–14; cf. 2 Kings 17:16–18), and He also rebuked the ancient Babylonians for trying to bypass His power through their "many sorceries" and "potent spells" (Isaiah 47:8–15).

Furthermore, occultists employ spiritualistic practices (mediumship) in order to contact nonphysical entities, including the souls of the dead. They believe that these spirits are capable of providing cosmic insights into this world and the next. Spiritists use Ouija boards, crystal balls, and the belongings of the dead to call on the departed. God's warning against those who practice spiritism couldn't be more ominous or direct: "I will set my face against the person who turns to mediums and spiritists to prostitute himself by following them, and I will cut him off from his people" (Leviticus 20:6; cf. 19:31; 1 Chronicles 10:13–14; Isaiah 8:19).

Finally, occultists try to access secret or hidden information about the future through soothsaying (divination). Common tools used by soothsayers include Tarot cards, astrological charts, horoscopes, and tea leaves.

The Lord's command is emphatic and explicit: "Do not practice divination" (Leviticus 19:26). It's a great insult to the power and providence of the Almighty to seek guidance through the occult. When the Israelites were about to enter the Promised Land, the Lord warned them not to imitate the detestable ways of the nations there: "Let no one be found among you who sacrifices his son or daughter in the fire, who practices divination or sorcery, interprets omens, engages in witchcraft, or casts spells, or who is a medium or spiritist or who consults the dead. Anyone who does these things is detestable to the Lord" (Deuteronomy 18:10–12; cf. Acts 13:6–11; 16:16–18; Galatians 5:19–21).

ACTS 19:18–20

"Many of those who believed now came and openly confessed their evil deeds. A number who had practiced sorcery brought their scrolls together and burned them publicly. When they calculated the value of the scrolls, the total came to fifty thousand drachmas. In this way the word of the Lord spread widely and grew in power."

For further study, see Elliot Miller, *A Crash Course on the New Age Movement* (Grand Rapids: Baker, 1989).

The objective
of occultism is
self-deification
through sorcery,
spiritism, and
soothsaying.

What Is the New Age Movement?

✳

N ot everyone who wears a cross is a
Christian. Likewise, not everyone who
owns a crystal is a New Ager. To accurately
identify New Agers, we have to move beyond
superficial symbols like crystals, unicorns, and
rainbows to identify their beliefs and practices.

First, New Agers practice "pantheistic monism"—
the view that God is all, all is God, and all is one.
They also believe that the universe operates under the
law of karma and its upshot, reincarnation.

Furthermore, the goal of New Agers is to
spiritually evolve and tap into their human potential
through the help of "ascended masters," or spirit
guides. To reach this level of enlightenment, New
Agers engage in occult practices like astrology, magic,
psychic healing, out-of-body experiences, and
meditation. In New Age meditation, for example, the
goal is to stamp out the self—and to become one
with the impersonal cosmic consciousness of the
universe. In sharp contrast, biblical meditation seeks
to center oneself on the personal Creator of the

universe—and it does so by focusing on Scripture (Joshua 1:8).

New Agers also share the vision of a coming "age of Aquarius" that's marked by global peace, prosperity, and planetary transformation. Their goal is summed up in catchphrases like "global village" and "planetary consciousness." Far from being an organized group, however, the New Age movement is a network of organizations like *Planetary Initiative for the World*, *Divine Light Mission*, and *Self-Realization Fellowship*—loosely linked, yet autonomous.

DEUTERONOMY 18:9–12

"When you enter the land the LORD your God is giving you, do not learn to imitate the detestable ways of the nations there. Let no one be found among you who sacrifices his son or daughter in the fire, who practices divination or sorcery, interprets omens, engages in witchcraft, or casts spells, or who is a medium or spiritist or who consults the dead. Anyone who does these things is detestable to the LORD."

For further study, see Douglas R. Groothuis, *Unmasking the New Age* (Downers Grove, Ill.: InterVarsity Press, 1986); for a comprehensive work, see Elliot Miller, *A Crash Course on the New Age Movement* (Grand Rapids: Baker Book House, 1989).

What's Wrong with Astrology?

s Charles Strohmer once put it so well, "Astrology has been debunked more than the tooth fairy and cheered more than the Pope." Despite the fact that it's condemned by Scripture, debunked by science, and obviously superstitious, our fascination with astrology continues to grow. While many see astrology as a harmless pastime, in reality it's a rigged "game" full of self-validating prophecies and a dangerous form of divination.

First, Scripture clearly condemns astrology as a practice that is "detestable to the LORD" (Deuteronomy 18:10–12). Isaiah goes so far as to say that the counsel of the "astrologers" and "stargazers who make predictions month by month" not only wore out the Babylonians but couldn't save them from their future ruin (Isaiah 47:13–14). Despite this clear condemnation of Scripture, there are people who argue that there's a biblical precedent for using stars to chart the future. For example, they talk about the star that guided the

Magi to the Messiah. But a quick look at context shows us that this star wasn't used to *foretell* the future, but to *forth tell* the future. In other words, the star of Bethlehem didn't *prophesy* the birth of Christ; it *pronounced* it (Matthew 2:9–10).

Furthermore, science has debunked astrology as a pseudoscience based on the odd belief that *galaxies* rather than *genes* determine inherited human characteristics. Not only that, astrology can't account for the problem posed by mass tragedies and twins. People with a wide variety of horoscopes all perished on 9/11. And twins born under the same sign of the zodiac often end up leading very different lives. Even King Nebuchadnezzar's astrologers recognized the weakness of their craft. When Nebuchadnezzar asked them to remind him of his dream and then interpret it, they responded in terror, saying, "There is not a man on earth who can do what the king asks!" (Daniel 2:10).

Finally, astrology undermines the natural use of the stars, which God ordains, for a superstitious use, which He disdains. Genesis 1:14 points to the natural use of the stars to separate day from the night, to serve as signs that mark seasons, days, and years, and to illuminate the earth. They also can rightly be used for purposes ranging from navigation to natural revelation. Thus, sailors may use astronavigation to chart their course; however, saints may not use astrology to chart their careers.

ISAIAH 47:13–15

"Let your astrologers come forward,
those stargazers who make predictions month
by month, let them save you from what is coming
upon you. Surely they are like stubble;
the fire will burn them up. They cannot
even save themselves from the power of the flame....
Each of them goes on in his error; there is
not one that can save you."

For further study, see Charles R. Strohmer, *America's Fascination with Astrology: Is It Healthy?* (Greenville, SC: Emerald House, 1998).

While many see astrology
as a harmless pastime,
in reality it's a rigged "game"
full of self-validating prophecies and
a dangerous form of divination.

Quite a few Christian leaders today hail Bible Codes as important evidence for the inspiration of Scripture, claiming that post-prophecies such as Israeli Prime Minister Yitzhak Rabin's assassination in 1995 are encoded in the biblical text. But in reality, Bible Codes are little more than a fringe variety of Jewish mysticism, repackaged for Christians.

First, like its older version, Bible Numerics, Bible Codes are at best a pseudoscience. Codes are "discovered" by searching for equidistant letter sequences (ELS) that can be compiled into intelligible messages pertaining to past events. One can search left to right, right to left, top to bottom, bottom to top, or in diagonal directions. Although sequencing can vary from word to word, none of the prophecies can be known *beforehand*. Like Monday-morning quarterbacking, hindsight is always perfect.

Furthermore, Bible Codes are a rigged game, complete with after-the-fact prophecies and self-validating messages. While ELS practitioners say that historical events like the assassination of Rabin are encoded in the Torah, nothing could be farther from the truth. Because Old Testament Hebrew doesn't contain vowels, an alleged code such as "Rabin Bang Bang" could just as easily refer to Christopher Robin's shooting his pop gun at the balloons Winnie the Pooh was holding when he floated over the Hundred Acre Wood ("Robin Bang Bang"). The self-validating message could also refer to the tire blowout that Batman's sidekick Robin experienced while riding in the Batmobile. It could even refer to a Mafia hitman name Robino who had two successful kills—bang, bang.

Finally, though the message of the *autographa* (original texts of the Bible) is unaltered in the best available manuscript copies, minor differences in spelling and style make it impossible to prove divine inspiration through equidistant letter sequencing. These kinds of minor discrepancies leave the meaning unaltered, but they completely undermine all attempts to find equidistant letter sequences by changing the distance between letters. In short, the coincidences found in equidistant letter sequences in the Torah aren't unique. They occur in every other work of literature from Homer to Hobbes and from Tolkien to Tolstoy.

Bible Codes shift the focus of biblical apologetics from the essential core of the gospel to esoteric speculations. In other words, anyone who denies that Jesus rose from the dead isn't likely to be persuaded by the pseudo-apologetics of Bible Codes.

LUKE 16:31

"If they do not listen to Moses and the Prophets,
they will not be convinced
even if someone rises from the dead."

For further study, see Hank Hanegraaff, "Magic Apologetics," *Christian Research Journal* 20, 1 (1997), available through the Christian Research Institute (CRI) at www.equip.org.

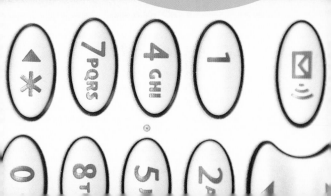

Bible Codes shift the
focus of biblical apologetics
from the essential core
of the gospel to
esoteric speculations.

Is There a Gospel in the Stars?

✳

O ver the years, I've observed an alarming trend toward what I call "magic apologetics." In place of an emphasis on such great apologetic truths as Creation, Christ's resurrection, and the inspiration of Scripture, we're being bombarded with a number of apologetic pretenders. One of the more curious brands of magic apologetics circulating through the Christian community is called the gospel in the stars (GIS). This apologetic posits that God from the beginning wrote the unique message of the gospel in the signs of the zodiac. At first glance, this magic apologetic may appear to have merit; closer examination, however, reveals a counterfeit.

First, GIS compromises the formal principle of the Reformation, namely, *sola Scriptura*. While *sola Scriptura* doesn't claim that the Bible is the sole source of revelation, it does hold that the Bible is the only infallible rule of faith and practice, the sole infallible storehouse of redemptive revelation. The Bible never gives an indication that God has

given us two infallible sources of special revelation—
the gospel in the stars and the gospel in the Scriptures.
GIS wasn't used by the prophets, the apostles,
Jesus Christ, or the early church as an apologetic
for the gospel.

Furthermore, GIS confuses special revelation
with general revelation. The church has always
understood the Bible to make a distinction between
general and special revelation. General revelation
proclaims the glory of God through order and
design (Psalm 19:1). Special revelation is found in
the "law of the LORD" inscribed in the pages of
Scripture (Psalm 19:7). From the *lights* we gain an
unspoken knowledge of the Creator; from the *Law*
we find salvation for our souls. Common sense
should suffice to tell us that while the heavens declare
the glory of God, they don't provide us with specific
salvific content. A common person looking at the
night sky would be hard-pressed to see the gospel in
the zodiac.

Finally, GIS subverts the natural use of the stars
for a superstitious use. The natural use of the stars is
to "separate the day from the night, and. . . serve as
signs to mark seasons and days and years, and. . .give
light on the earth" (Genesis 1:14–15). Stars can also
be rightly used for varied purposes ranging from

natural revelation to navigation. Indeed, "The heavens declare the glory of God; the skies proclaim the work of his hands. Day after day they pour forth speech; night after night they display knowledge. There is no speech or language where their voice is not heard. Their voice goes out into all the earth, their words to the ends of the world" (Psalm 19:1–4).

Because GIS compromises *sola Scriptura*, confuses special revelation with general revelation, and promotes superstition, it would benefit Christians to reject it and return to genuine apologetic arguments. Every Christian should be equipped to communicate the evidence that God created the universe, that Jesus Christ proved He was God through the resurrection, and that the Bible is divine rather than just human in origin.

GENESIS 1:14–15

"And God said, 'Let there be lights in the expanse of the sky to separate the day from the night, and let them serve as signs to mark seasons and days and years, and let them be lights in the expanse of the sky to give light on the earth.' And it was so."

For further study, see Charles Strohmer, "Is There a Christian Zodiac, a Gospel in the Stars?" *Christian Research Journal* 22, 4 (2000), available through the Christian Research Institute (CRI) at www.equip.org.

Common sense should suffice to tell us that while the heavens declare the glory of God, they don't provide us with specific salvific content.

Is Baptism Necessary for Salvation?

✳

T hose who think baptism is necessary for salvation often quote Peter in Acts 2:38— "Repent and be baptized"—as evidence that belief *plus* baptism results in salvation. Scripture clearly doesn't support this view.

First, as the book of Acts demonstrates, baptism is a *sign* of conversion, not the *means* of conversion. Indeed, Acts 10:47 describes believers who were indwelt by the Holy Spirit (and therefore saved— see Romans 8:9) prior to being baptized. When the thief on the cross placed his faith in Christ, Jesus said to him, "Today you will be with me in paradise" (Luke 23:43), even though the dying thief had no chance to be baptized.

As a whole, the Bible clearly says that we're saved by faith and not by works (Ephesians 2:8–9). As Paul points out in Romans, our righteous standing before God is "by faith from first to last" (Romans 1:17). When the jailer asked the apostle Paul, "What must I do to be saved?" Paul responded,

"Believe in the Lord Jesus, and you will be saved" (Acts 16:30–31).

Although baptism isn't the way that we're saved, it *is* the way that we're set apart. It's through baptism that we proclaim we're no longer our own—we've been bought by Christ's blood and brought into the community of faith. In Acts 2:38, Peter wasn't suggesting that his hearers couldn't be saved apart from baptism; instead, he was saying that their genuine repentance would be evidenced by their baptism. As Saint Augustine wrote, it's not the absence of baptism but the despising of baptism that damns.

Behind the symbol of baptism is the *substance* of baptism—the blood of Jesus Christ, which cleanses us from sin. Just like water removes soil and sweat from the skin, so the blood of Jesus Christ removed the stain of sin from our souls.

GALATIANS 3:26–27

"You are all sons of God through faith in Christ Jesus, for all of you who were baptized into Christ have clothed yourselves with Christ."

For further study, see Hank Hanegraaff, "Bringing Baptism into Biblical Balance," *Christian Research Journal*, vol. 19, no. 1 (1996), available through the Christian Research Institute at www.equip.org.

Does the Book of James Teach That We're Saved by Works?

✳

C ritics of the Bible have argued for a while now that the book of James contradicts the rest of Scripture in teaching "that a person is justified by what he does and not by faith alone" (James 2:24). If you examine James closely, though, you'll see that it agrees with the rest of the Bible that we aren't saved by what we do but by what Jesus Christ has done.

Read in context, James doesn't teach that we're saved by works but by the kind of faith that produces good works. As James puts it, "What good is it, my brothers, if a man claims to have faith but has no deeds? Can such faith save him?" (v. 14). The answer is no: "As the body without the spirit is dead, so faith without deeds is dead" (v. 26).

And when James says that a person isn't justified by faith alone, he means that a person isn't justified by mental *assent* alone. "Show me your faith without deeds, and I will show you my faith by what I do. You believe that there is one God. Good!

Even the demons believe that—and shudder" (vv. 18–19). In other words, demons believe in the sense of giving mental *assent* to the fact that there is only one true God, all the while failing to place their hope and trust in Him.

When James says, "A person is justified by what he does and not by faith alone," and Paul says, "Man is justified by faith apart from observing the law" (Romans 3:28), their words are in complete harmony. James is countering the false claim that a *stated faith* is a substitute for a *saving faith*, while Paul is countering the equally wrong notion that salvation can be earned by observing the Law alone. As the Reformers were known to say, "Justification is by faith alone, but not by a faith that is alone."

JAMES 2:21–22

"Was not our ancestor Abraham considered righteous for what he did when he offered his son Isaac on the altar? You see that his faith and his actions were working together, and his faith was made complete by what he did."

For further study, see R. C. Sproul, *Justified by Faith Alone* (Wheaton, Ill.: Crossway Books, 1999).

– 70 –

Can a Non-Christian Be Saved by Marrying a Christian?

✳

I n his first letter to the Corinthian Christians, Paul writes that "the unbelieving husband has been sanctified through his wife, and the unbelieving wife has been sanctified through her husband" (7:14). Does this mean that unbelievers are saved through being married to believers?

First, if unbelievers can be saved through marriage, there would be at least two ways to be saved: one by God's grace through faith in Jesus Christ alone, and the other by marriage to a believer. Not only so, but unbelievers would be forced into the kingdom of Christ against their wills.

Furthermore, being *sanctified* isn't the same as being *saved*. To be *sanctified* means to be set apart. As such, the unbeliever has been sanctified for the sake of the marriage, not the sake of salvation. In other words, the believer isn't defiled by the spiritual deadness of the unbeliever. Rather, the unbeliever comes under the special influence of the Holy Spirit.

Finally, in the self-same context, Paul distinguishes between being sanctified and being saved by writing: "How do you know, wife, whether you will *save* your husband? Or, how do you know, husband, whether you will *save* your wife?" (v. 16, emphasis added). It's important to understand that sanctification isn't the same thing as salvation.

*"Jesus answered, 'I am the way and
the truth and the life. No one comes to the Father
except through me.'"*

For further study, see Gordon Fee and Douglas Stewart, *How to Read the Bible for All Its Worth*, 3rd ed. (Grand Rapids: Zondervan, 2003).

Do Women Really Have to Be Silent in Church?

✳

he following words by the apostle Paul are frequently used to label the Bible as sexist: "I do not permit a woman to teach or to have authority over a man; *she must be silent.* For Adam was formed first, then Eve. And Adam was not the one deceived; it was the woman who was deceived and became a sinner" (1 Timothy 2:12–14, emphasis added). Through a careful consideration of context, the assertion that Paul's teaching is sexist is silenced.

First, Paul obviously isn't saying that women must always be silent in church. Rather, in a culture in which women were largely illiterate and unlearned, Paul is saying that until a woman *learns*, she shouldn't presume to teach. If Paul had intended to say a woman must always be silent, he wouldn't have given women instructions on how to pray or prophesy publicly in church (1 Corinthians 11:5).

Furthermore, by referring to Eve's deception in the garden, Paul is drawing readers' attention to how crucial it is that women, like men, involve themselves in learning. Far from chastising Eve for her role in the Fall, Paul chastises the Jewish men of his day for excluding women from learning, which left them easy prey for deception. Just as Adam was responsible for failing to protect Eve from deception, so too the men of Paul's day would be responsible if they kept women from studying and growing in their faith.

Finally, Paul's words here refute the matriarchal authoritarianism practiced by pagan cults in that day. The city of Ephesus, where Timothy ministered, was home to a cult dedicated to the pagan goddess Artemis. Worship of Artemis took place under the authority of an entirely female priesthood that exercised authoritarian dominion over male worshipers. Thus, Paul emphasizes that women shouldn't presume undue authority over men. Paul neither elevates women over men nor men over women, but he is concerned that men and women be granted equal opportunity to learn and grow in submission to one another and to God (1 Timothy 2:11; cf. Ephesians 5:21).

Ephesians 5:21

"Submit to one another out of reverence for Christ."

For further study, see N. T. Wright, "Women's Service in the Church: The Biblical Basis," available online at www.ntwrightpage.com.

Liberal scholars today are advancing the notion that the New Testament's canonization was driven by anti-Semitic motives. In fact, it has become popular to assert that the story of Judas's betrayal of Christ was invented because "Judas" allegedly meant "Jew." In reality, anti-Semitism had nothing to do with the canonization of the New Testament. Early dating, eyewitness attestation, and extra-biblical corroboration did!

First, it's obvious to any unbiased person that the New Testament is anything but anti-Semitic. Jesus, the twelve apostles, and the apostle Paul were all Jewish! In fact, Christians proudly refer to their heritage as the Judeo-Christian tradition. In the book of Hebrews, Christians are reminded of Jews, from David to Daniel, who are members of the "faith hall of fame." Christian children grow up with Jews as their heroes!

Furthermore, New Testament writers clearly proclaimed that salvation through the Jewish Messiah was given first to the Jewish people and then to the rest of the world (Matthew 15:24;

Romans 1:16). Additionally, Peter's vision followed by Cornelius's receiving the Holy Spirit (Acts 10) and the subsequent Jerusalem council (Acts 15) clearly show both the inclusive nature of the church as well as the initial Jewish Christian resistance to Gentile inclusion (see also Galatians 2:11–14). While the early Christians were certainly not anti-Semitic, at least some Jewish believers initially manifested the opposite prejudice. Far from being anti-Semitic, the New Testament simply records the outworking of redemption history as foretold by the Jewish prophets who prophesied that one of Christ's companions would betray Him (Psalm 41:9; John 13:18). There's nothing subtle about the crucifixion narrative. The Jewish Gospel writers explicitly state that it was their leaders who condemned Christ of blasphemy. There would be no motive to fabricate a fictional Judas to represent the model Jew.

Finally, Scripture as a whole goes to great lengths to emphasize that when it comes to faith in Jesus, there's no distinction between Jew and Gentile (Galatians 3:28) and that Jewish people throughout the generations are no more responsible for Christ's death than anyone else. As Ezekiel puts it, "The son will not share the guilt of the father, nor will the father share the guilt of the son" (Ezekiel 18:20). The truth is that liberal scholars owe the world an apology for inventing a brand of fundamentalism that encourages bigotry and hatred by spreading the absurd idea that the New Testament is anti-Semitic.

ROMANS 1:16

"I am not ashamed of the gospel, because it is the power of God for the salvation of everyone who believes: first for the Jew, then for the Gentiles."

For further study, see Hank Hanegraaff, "The Search for Jesus Hoax," *Christian Research Journal* 23, 2 (2000), available through the Christian Research Institute (CRI) at www.equip.org.

Far from being anti-Semitic, the New Testament simply records the outworking of redemption history as foretold by the Jewish prophets who prophesied that one of Christ's companions would betray Him.

Is Speaking in Tongues *the* Evidence of the Baptism of the Holy Spirit?

※

I t has become increasingly common for Christians to suppose that the full gospel includes the baptism of the Holy Spirit with the evidence of speaking in tongues. Thus the question: Is speaking in tongues *the* evidence of being baptized by the Holy Spirit?

First, as the apostle Paul makes plain, believers are "all baptized by one Spirit into one body" (1 Corinthians 12:13), yet not all who believe speak in tongues (vv. 10, 30). In other words, tongues may be a manifestation of the baptism of the Holy Spirit, but tongues cannot be *the* manifestation.

Furthermore, even if a believer speaks in tongues, it isn't a guarantee that he has been baptized in the Holy Spirit. As Paul puts it, "If I speak in the tongues of men and of angels, but have not love, I am only a resounding gong or a clanging cymbal" (1 Corinthians 13:1). As Paul also says, without love, "I am nothing" (v. 2). I would also add that socio-psychological manipulation tactics like peer pressure or the subtle power of suggestion can encourage excited utterances that are not from the Spirit.

Finally, as Scripture makes clear, the truest sign of the baptism of the Holy Spirit isn't speaking in tongues; rather, it is confessing Jesus Christ as our Lord, repenting from sin, and obeying God (Romans 8:1–17; 1 John 4:12–16; cf. Ephesians 1:13–15). "Those who live in accordance with the Spirit have their minds set on what the Spirit desires. The mind of sinful man is death, but the mind controlled by the Spirit is life and peace" (Romans 8:5–6). As this verse indicates, the fruit of the Spirit isn't just speaking in tongues, but "love, joy, peace, patience, kindness, goodness, faithfulness, gentleness and self-control" (Galatians 5:22–23). Through this we see that righteousness, not tongues, is the core expression of Christianity.

EPHESIANS 5:18–21

*"Do not get drunk on wine,
which leads to debauchery. Instead, be filled
with the Spirit. Speak to one another with psalms,
hymns and spiritual songs. Sing and
make music in your heart to the Lord, always
giving thanks to God the Father for everything, in the
name of our Lord Jesus Christ. Submit to one
another out of reverence for Christ."*

For further study, see Hank Hanegraaff, "What Does It Mean to Say the Holy Spirit Is *in* You?" on p. 26

Righteousness,
not tongues, is the core expression
of Christianity.

How Old Will We Be in Heaven?

✳

S cripture doesn't specifically address the issue of age in heaven; however, it does provide some wonderful insights about the state of our resurrected bodies.

First, when God created Adam and Eve in Eden, He created them with apparent age and in the prime of life. Additionally, Jesus died and was resurrected at the prime of His physical development. Thus, we are justified in believing that whether we die in infancy, in our prime, or in old age, we'll be resurrected physically mature and perfect, just as God originally intended.

Furthermore, our DNA is programmed in such a way that at a particular point we reach ideal development from a perspective of function. For the most part, it appears that we reach this stage somewhere in our twenties or thirties. Prior to this stage, the development of our bodies (anabolism) is greater than the devolution of our bodies (catabolism). From this point on, the rate of breakdown exceeds the rate of buildup, which eventually leads to physical death. All of this is to say that if the blueprint for our glorified bodies is in the DNA, then it would stand to reason that our bodies will be resurrected at the optimal stage of development determined by our DNA.

Finally, one thing can be stated with certainty—in heaven, there will be no deformities. Our bodies, tarnished by humanity's fall into a life of constant sin that ends in death, will be utterly transformed. You will be the perfect you, and I'll be the perfect me. In heaven, "there will be no more death or mourning or crying or pain, for the old order of things has passed away" (Revelation 21:4).

ISAIAH 35:5–6
"Then will the eyes of the blind be opened and the ears of the deaf unstopped. Then will the lame leap like a deer, and the mute tongue shout for joy. Water will gush forth in the wilderness and streams in the desert."

For further study, see Peter J. Kreeft, *Everything You Ever Wanted to Know about Heaven, but Never Dreamed of Asking* (San Francisco: Ignatius Press, 1980).

Will There Be Sex in Heaven?

※

What do you think of when the word *sex* is mentioned? An image of Jessica Simpson? A Brad Pitt movie? *Cosmopolitan* magazine? Or does your mind immediately flash from sex to Scripture? Trust me, when it comes to valuing sex, *Playboy* magazine can't hold a candle to Scripture. If you think that's an overstatement, just read a few pages of Solomon's Song of Songs.

Sadly, what our Creator designed to be precious and pure, the creation has prostituted and perverted. But that isn't where the story ends. God doesn't arbitrarily take things away; rather, He *redeems* them.

So will there be sex in the resurrection? The answer is yes—and no. It all depends on what you mean by sex.

First, by nature or essence we are sexual beings. Therefore, sex isn't something we do; it's what we *are*. The reason I can say that there will certainly be sex in the resurrection is that sex isn't merely a word describing an erotic experience; it is actually what we are—in the beginning God created us male and female (Genesis 1:27), and that is likely how it will always be.

Furthermore, we can safely assume that there will be *sexuality* in heaven because heaven will personify enjoyment. Men and women will enjoy each other—not in a mere physical sense, but also in a metaphysical sense. This reality is virtually impossible for a crass materialist to understand. The world views sexual pleasure as a function of fitting body parts together. Christians, however, see humanity as a unity of both body and soul. As a result, we're not merely sexual bodies; we're sexual souls as well. In heaven, the pleasure that the male and female sex will experience in one another will be magnified infinitely, because in eternity our earthly conception of sex will have been eclipsed. In place of selfishness, we'll take pleasure in selflessness.

Finally, we can be assured that there will be sex in eternity because God created sex in Eden—*before* humanity's fall into a life of constant sin terminated by death. Thus, in Eden Restored we can be sure that God won't *remove* our sexual nature, but rather *redeem* it. In the new heaven and new earth, sex will no longer be for the purpose of procreation, nor will it involve sexual intercourse—for "at the resurrection people will neither marry nor be given in marriage;

they will be like the angels in heaven" (Matthew 22:30). In heaven we'll experience a kind of spiritual intercourse that we can't even grasp here on earth. In paradise, romance will be perfect. It will be agape-driven rather than animal-driven. In Eden Restored, our sexual bodies and sexual souls will fly full and free, unrestrained by selfishness and sin.

Will there be sex in the resurrection? Again, yes and no. Yes, there will be *sexuality* in heaven because *we'll* be in heaven—we, by our very nature, are sexual beings. And no, there is no reason to believe that there will be sex in heaven in terms of the physical act.

GENESIS 1:27

"So God created man in his own image,
in the image of God he created him; male and
female he created them."

For further study, see Hank Hanegraaff, *Resurrection* (Nashville: Word Publishing), chapter 17. See also Peter J. Kreeft, *Everything You Ever Wanted to Know about Heaven, but Never Dreamed of Asking* (San Francisco: Ignatius Press, 1990).

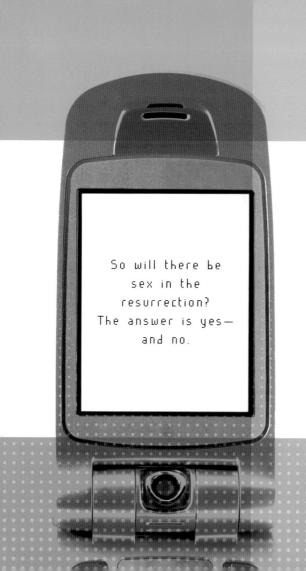

– 7 6 –

Will There Be Animals in Heaven?

✳

Scripture doesn't conclusively tell us whether our pets will make it to heaven. However, the Bible does provide us with some significant clues about whether or not animals will inhabit the new heaven and the new earth.

First, animals populated the Garden of Eden, so there's a precedent for believing that animals will populate Eden Restored as well. Animals are among God's most creative creations, and it would seem incredible that He would banish such wonders in heaven.

Furthermore, while we can't say for certain that the pets we enjoy today will be "resurrected" in eternity, I'm not willing to eliminate it as a possibility. Some of the keenest thinkers—from C. S. Lewis to Peter Kreeft—are convinced that not just animals in general, but pets in particular, will be restored in the resurrection. If God resurrected our pets, it would be in total keeping with His overwhelming grace and goodness.

Finally, the Scriptures suggest that animals have souls. Both Moses in Genesis and John in Revelation communicate that the Creator endowed animals with souls. In the original languages of Genesis 1:20 and Revelation 8:9, *nephesh* and *psyche* respectively refer to the essence of life or soul. Not until Descartes and Hobbes and the Enlightenment did people think otherwise about animals. However, because the soul of an animal is qualitatively different from the soul of a human, there is reasonable doubt that it can survive the death of its body.

One thing is for sure: Scripture provides us with sufficient evidence for believing that animals will inhabit the new heaven and new earth. In the words of Isaiah: "The wolf will live with the lamb, the leopard will lie down with the goat, the calf and the lion and the yearling together; and a little child will lead them" (Isaiah 11:6).

PSALM 145:13
"Your kingdom is an everlasting kingdom,
and your dominion endures through all generations.
The LORD is faithful to all his promises and
loving toward all he has made."

For further study, see Hank Hanegraaff, *Resurrection* (Nashville: Word Publishing, 2000), chapter 13.

Are There Degrees of Reward in Heaven?

✳

D egrees of reward in heaven aren't usually the subject of today's sermons. They were, however, a constant theme in Jesus' sermons—and He talked specifically about *degrees* of reward that will be given for faithful service, self-sacrifice, and suffering. Scripture is full of references to rewards. While we're saved by God's grace through faith in Jesus Christ alone, what we do now counts for all eternity.

First, it's significant to note that in His most famous sermon, Christ repeatedly referred to rewards. In concluding the Beatitudes, He said, "Blessed are you when people insult you, persecute you and falsely say all kinds of evil against you because of me. Rejoice and be glad, because great is your *reward* in heaven" (Matthew 5:11–12, emphasis added). Christ continued His message by warning the crowd that if they did their acts of righteousness to be seen by men, they wouldn't receive a reward in heaven (6:1–6, 16–18). Christ's message is crystal clear: rather than focus on earthly goals like the admiration of others, we should focus on things that are eternal, like the approval of our Father. Jesus encouraged His followers to store up "treasures in heaven, where moth and rust do not destroy, and where thieves do not break in and steal" (6:20).

Christ often included the same lesson in His parables. In the parable of the talents (Matthew 25:14–30), Jesus told the story of a man who entrusted his property to his servants before going on a long journey. Each servant received an amount equal to his abilities. To one servant he gave five talents, to another two talents, and to a third he gave one. The servant who received five talents doubled his money, and so did the servant who received two. The last servant, however, buried his master's money in the ground. When the master returned, he rewarded the faithful servants with the words, "Well done, good and faithful servant! You have been faithful with a few things; I will put you in charge of many things. Come and share your master's happiness!" (v. 23). The silly servant who buried his talents not only forfeited his reward, but he was thrown into outer darkness, "where there will be weeping and gnashing of teeth"(v. 30).

Scripture also communicates degrees of reward in the resurrection. The basis of our salvation is the finished work of Christ, but Christians can erect a building of rewards upon that foundation. As Paul puts it, "No one can lay any foundation other than the one already laid, which is Jesus Christ. If any man builds on this foundation using gold, silver, costly stones, wood, hay or straw, his work will be shown for what it is, because the Day will bring it to light. It will be revealed with fire, and the fire will test the quality of each man's work. If what he has built survives, he will receive his reward. If it is burned up, he will suffer loss; he himself will be saved, but only as one escaping through the flames" (1 Corinthians 3:11–15).

Paul shows us in these verses how some Christians will be resurrected with very little to show for the time they spent on earth—they "will be saved, but only as one escaping through the flames." This brings up the image of people escaping from burning buildings with no more than the charred clothes upon their backs. This will be the case for even the most visible Christian leaders whose motives were selfish rather than selfless.

On the other hand, people who build selflessly upon the foundation of Christ using "gold, silver and costly stones" will receive enduring rewards. Selfless Christians who work hard without recognition will hear the words they long for: "Well done, good and faithful servant! You have been faithful with a few things; I will put you in charge of many things. Come and share your master's happiness!" (Matthew 25:21). While good deeds are part of our duty as Christians, not even the smallest act of kindness will go without its reward.

Finally, degrees of reward in eternity involve both greater responsibilities as well as greater spiritual capacities. An experience I had several years ago taught me this. I received an invitation to play golf at Cypress Point, arguably the most spectacular golf course on the planet. Let me tell you, I have rarely worked so hard for anything in my life! For months I beat my body into submission. I lifted weights, worked on stretching exercises, and pounded thousands of golf balls, all the while dreaming about the day I would walk the fairways of Cypress Point. Without my tough preparation, I would have still experienced the same cliffside vistas and breathtaking views. I would still have been able to smell the fragrance of the Monterey cypresses and feel the refreshing sting of the salt air upon my face. All my hard work, however, added greatly to the final experience.

That's how heaven will be! Just like a master musician can appreciate Mozart more than can your average music lover, so my strenuous training allowed me to more fully appreciate the experience of golfing at Cypress Point. And let me tell you, as phenomenal as Cypress Point is, it pales in comparison to what Paradise will be. I spent one day at a golf haven; I will spend an eternity in God's heaven.

It stands to reason, then, that we should put a whole lot more effort into preparing for an eternity in heaven with God than I did for playing eighteen holes of golf. And that's precisely the point Paul is driving at in his first letter to the Corinthians: "Do you not know that in a race all the runners run, but only one gets the prize? Run in such a way as to get the prize. Everyone who competes in the games goes into strict training. They do it to get a crown that will not last; but we do it to get a crown that will last forever" (9:24–25). Paul also writes, "I do not run like a man running aimlessly; I do not fight like a man beating the air. No, I beat my body and make it my slave so that after I have preached to others, I myself will not be disqualified for the prize" (vv. 26–27).

*"For we must all appear before the
judgment seat of Christ, that each one may receive
what is due him for the things done while
in the body, whether good or bad."*

For further study, see Hank Hanegraaff, *Resurrection* (Nashville: Word Publishing, 2000).

— 7 8 —

Why Should I Believe in Hell?

✳

The horrors of hell are so great that they cause us to instinctively react in disbelief and doubt. Yet there are compelling reasons that should cause us to erase such doubt from our minds.

First, Christ, the creator of the cosmos, clearly communicated how real hell is. He spent more time talking about hell than He did about heaven. In the Sermon on the Mount alone (Matthew 5–7), He explicitly warned His followers about the dangers of hell a half dozen or more times. In the Olivet Discourse (Matthew 24–25), Christ repeatedly warned His followers of the judgment that is to come. And in His famous story of the Rich Man and Lazarus (Luke 16), Christ gave us a detailed description of the finality of eternal torment in hell.

Furthermore, the concept of choice demands that we believe in hell. Without hell, there is no choice. And without choice, heaven wouldn't be heaven; heaven would be hell. The righteous would inherit a counterfeit heaven, and the unrighteous would be incarcerated in heaven against their wills, which would be a torture worse than hell. Imagine spending a lifetime voluntarily distanced from God, only to find yourself involuntarily dragged into His loving presence for all eternity; the alternative to hell is worse than hell itself, in that humans made in the image of God would be stripped of freedom and forced to worship God against their will.

Finally, common sense dictates that there must be a hell. Without hell, the wrongs of Hitler's Holocaust will never be righted. Justice would be mocked if, after slaughtering six million Jews, Hitler merely died in the arms of his mistress with no eternal consequences. The ancients knew better than to think such a thing. David knew that for a while it might seem like the wicked prosper in spite of their deeds, but in the end justice will be served.

Common sense also dictates that without a hell there is no need for a Savior. We don't even need to say more about how ridiculous it is to suggest that the Creator should suffer more than He already has—i.e., the cumulative sufferings of all of mankind—if there were no hell to save us from.

Without hell, there's no need for salvation. Without salvation, there's no need for a sacrifice. And without sacrifice, there's no need for a Savior. As much as we might want to think that everyone will be saved, common sense rules out that possibility.

DANIEL 12:2

> *"Multitudes who sleep in the dust of the earth*
> *will awake: some to everlasting life,*
> *others to shame and everlasting contempt."*

For further study, see Hank Hanegraaff, *Resurrection* (Nashville: Word Publishing, 2000), chapter 7.

The concept
of choice demands
that we
believe in hell.

Are There Degrees of Punishment in Hell?

B ased on what the Bible tells us, it's safe to say that not all existence in hell is equal.

First, Scripture unquestionably tells us that God is perfectly just and will reward and punish each person in accordance with what he or she has done (see Psalm 62:12; Proverbs 24:12; Jeremiah 17:10; Ezekiel 18:20, 30; Romans 2:5–16; 1 Corinthians 3:8, 11–15; 2 Corinthians 5:10; Colossians 3:23–25; 1 Peter 1:17; Revelation 20:12).

Furthermore, the Bible clearly explains that along with greater revelation and responsibility comes stricter judgment (cf. James 3:1). Jesus warned the Pharisees that they would "be punished most severely" for their willful hypocrisy (Luke 20:47). In denouncing the cities where most of His miracles were performed, Jesus said, "Woe to you, Korazin! Woe to you, Bethsaida! If the miracles that were performed in you had been performed in Tyre and Sidon, they would have repented long ago in sackcloth and ashes" (Matthew 11:21). Jesus then said, "It will be more bearable for Tyre and Sidon on the day of judgment than for you" (v. 22).

And Jesus used the metaphor of physical torture to warn that those who knowingly disobey will experience greater torment in hell than those who disobey in ignorance (Luke 12:47–48).

Finally, Scripture confirms the common-sense idea that not all sins are created equal (cf. John 19:11). For example, to think a murderous thought is sin, but to carry that thought out in reality is far more serious. Every sin is an act of rebellion against a holy God, but some sins carry more consequence than others, and thus deserve severer punishment—both in this life and the next. According to Scripture, the torment of Hitler's hell will greatly exceed that of the less wicked.

REVELATION 20:12

"And I saw the dead, great and small,
standing before the throne, and books were opened.
Another book was opened, which is the book
of life. The dead were judged according to
what they had done as recorded in the books."

For further study, see Hank Hanegraaff, "Why Should I Believe in Hell?" and "Is Annihilationism Biblical?" *The Bible Answer Book Volume 1* (Nashville: J. Countryman, 2004), 211–18.

– 80 –

What Does 666 Mean?

Many people today believe that the number "666" represents a modern-day beast about to be revealed. Placing that beast in the twenty-first century, however, could well pose serious difficulties.

First, John, the author of Revelation, told a first-century audience that with "wisdom" and "insight" they would be able to "calculate the number of the beast, for it is man's number. His number is 666" (Revelation 13:18). Obviously, no amount of wisdom and insight would have allowed a first-century audience to calculate the number of a twenty-first-century beast. It would have been cruel and dangerously misleading for John to suggest to first-century Christians that they would identify the beast if, in fact, the beast was a twenty-first-century individual or institution.

Furthermore, unlike today, transforming names into numbers was common in antiquity. For example, in *The Lives of the Twelve Caesars*, the Roman historian Suetonius identified Nero by a numerical designation equal to an evil deed. This number was encapsulated in the phrase "count the numerical values of the letters in Nero's name, and in 'murdered his own mother,' and you will find their sum is the same." In Greek, the numerical value of the letters in Nero's name totaled 1,005, and so did the numbers in the phrase "murdered his own mother." This ancient cryptogram reflected the widespread belief that Nero killed his own mother.

Finally, while "Nero" in Greek totaled 1,005, the reader of John's letter familiar with the Hebrew language could recognize that the Greek spelling of "Nero Caesar" transliterated into Hebrew equals 666. Moreover, the presence in some ancient manuscripts of a variation in which 666 is rendered 616 lends further credence to Nero as the intended. The Hebrew transliteration of the Latin spelling of "Nero Caesar" totals 616, just like the Hebrew transliteration of the Greek, which includes an additional letter (Greek: "v"=50, English transliteration: "n"=50), renders 666. Thus, two seemingly unrelated numbers lead you to the same doorstep—that of a beast named Nero Caesar.

Because of this reasoning, twenty-first-century believers—just like their first-century counterparts—can know for sure that 666 is the number of Nero's name; Nero is the Beast who ravaged the bride of Christ in a historical milieu that included three and a half years of persecution. In the end, Peter and Paul were both persecuted and put to death at the hands of this Beast. Indeed, this was the only time in human history when the Beast could directly attack the foundation of the Christian church, of which Christ Himself was the cornerstone.

REVELATION 13:18

*"This calls for wisdom. If anyone has insight,
let him calculate the number of the beast, for it is
man's number. His number is 666."*

For further study, see Hank Hanegraaff, *The Apocalypse Code* (Nashville: W Publishing Group, 2007).

Nero is the Beast who ravaged the bride of Christ.

Who Is the Antichrist?

✳

For centuries now, Christians have wondered about the identity of the Antichrist. Likely candidates have included past princes and popes, as well as present rulers and presidents. Rather than joining in on the sensationalistic game of Pin the Tail on the Antichrist, Christians should turn to Scripture for the answer.

First, the apostle John exposes the identity of the Antichrist when he writes, "Who is the liar? It is the man who denies that Jesus is the Christ. Such a man is the antichrist—he denies the Father and the Son. No one who denies the Son has the Father; whoever acknowledges the Son has the Father also" (1 John 2:22–23). In his second epistle, John gives a similar warning: "Many deceivers, who do not acknowledge Jesus Christ as coming in the flesh, have gone out into the world. Any such person is the deceiver and the antichrist" (1:7).

Furthermore, John taught that all who deny the incarnation, messianic role, and deity of Jesus are instances of antichrist. In this light, we see that the term *antichrist* refers to the apostasy not only of individuals but of institutions and ideologies as well. In this way, institutions like modern-day cults and world religions along with ideologies like evolutionism and communism can rightly be considered antichrist.

In the book of Revelation, John identifies both an individual and an institution that represent the ultimate personification of evil—the archetypal antichrist. He referred to it as a beast who "deceived the inhabitants of the earth" (Revelation 13:14). Drawing on Daniel's apocalyptic portrayal of evil world powers (Revelation 13; cf. Daniel 7–8), John wrote about an emperor in his own era who arrogantly sets himself and his empire against God (vv. 5–6), violently persecuting the saints (v. 7), and grossly violating the commandments through a long list of disgusting demonstrations of depravity, including his demand to be worshiped as Lord and God (vv. 8, 15).

1 JOHN 2:18–19

*"Dear children, this is the last hour;
and as you have heard that the antichrist is coming,
even now many antichrists have come.
This is how we know it is the last hour. They went
out from us, but they did not really belong to us.
For if they had belonged to us, they would
have remained with us; but their going
showed that none of them belonged to us."*

For further study, see "What Does 666 Mean?" on page 256; see also Hank Hanegraaff, *The Apocalypse Code* (Nashville: W Publishing Group, 2007).